Jamaican Ancestry

How To Find Out More

Revised Edition

Madeleine E. Mitchell

HERITAGE BOOKS
2008

HERITAGE BOOKS

AN IMPRINT OF HERITAGE BOOKS, INC.

Books, CDs, and more—Worldwide

For our listing of thousands of titles see our website
at
www.HeritageBooks.com

Published 2008 by
HERITAGE BOOKS, INC.
Publishing Division
100 Railroad Ave. #104
Westminster, Maryland 21157

Other books by the author:

Jamaican Ancestry: How To Find Out More

Selected Vital Records from the Jamaican Daily Gleaner*: Life on the
Island of Jamaica as Seen through Newspaper Extracts
Volume 1: 1865-1915
Volume 2: 1916-1939*

International Standard Book Numbers
Paperbound: 978-0-7884-4282-7
Clothbound: 978-0-7884-7712-6

For my mother Christine

Contents

Preface

While there have not been a great deal of new resources found since I wrote the first edition of this book, there are sufficient changes as to where sources can be found particularly on the internet to warrant an update to this book. In this edition I have tried to include where the reader can find sources of family history through on-line sources as well as books and other materials not referred to previously. One consideration for including the URL locators (the http://www. etc) of on-line sources is the ephemeral nature of some of the links, so that by the time this edition is published some of the links may no longer be valid. That is a risk I will have to take, but I have tried to minimize this by choosing those I have found to be more stable. Sometimes I have found that just the last file name has been changed and the researcher can find the new file by stepping back one or two slashes in the URL.

As I said in the first edition, I have assumed that the reader has some knowledge of basic family history research, but may be this is not the case. I recommend taking a course if there is one available from your local genealogical society even if it is not oriented towards Jamaica. Also there are many basic family history books in local libraries which would help to start the new researcher in the right direction. Often I get requests via e-mail as to how to start doing family research for Jamaica. On-line there are two sources I would recommend: http://www.genuki.org.uk/gs/ if you are in the United Kingdom and http://www.rootsweb.com/~rwguide/index.html which is more oriented towards the North American audiences. The latter URL also has links to show pedigrees, family group sheets and research logs which can demonstrate how to start documenting what you find on forms. Many computer programs (genealogical computing) have these forms as reports, so that once you enter the data you can print out these forms to have for your on-going research. After writing down all the known data of births, marriages and deaths of self, parents and grandparents, great-grandparents, most people will want to start with Civil Registration records to find information to fill in the gaps. This may involve Civil Registration in Jamaica, England and Canada and vital records in individual states in the U.S.

If you are going to use Civil Registration records from Jamaica (see chapter) it is vital that you know the parish or the likely parish in which the ancestor was located. There is no all island index to this source of birth, marriage and death records. And depending on the time period there were up to 22 parishes compared to the present 14 parishes (see maps), so knowing a location is a necessary prerequisite to finding a record for the family member.

I would like to thank particularly Dorothy Kew for suggestions in updating this book and for the many kind tributes she has made to others about the first edition.

Madeleine Mitchell
8900 SW 194th Court
Dunnellon, Florida, 34432-2795
March 8, 2006

Preface to the First Edition

I am a family historian who has been working on her Jamaican ancestry for 13 years. I have not found a handy guide for this work, so I thought it would be nice to put down on paper the sources I have found useful for those who are just beginning or are still looking for sources. In particular I think it might be useful to those Jamaicans who have immigrated to North America (Canada and the United States) and to England, but who believe there is not much they can do without access to records in Jamaica. Actually, there are many records that are available if you know how to access the various sources through libraries and other repositories. First however is to know "Wha d'a yah" (what is here). My ulterior motive is to spur the interest in genealogy of Jamaica so that more documents can be preserved and transferred to microform so that they are readily available. The tropics are so hard on paper and every natural disaster, hurricane and earthquake can take a few more sources which we depend on to trace our ancestors. The government of Jamaica has limited resources to put into preserving archival material when the real needs of people for everyday living are so pressing. I also hope that if the demand is generated, some books that are now out of print will be reprinted.

This book is not just for Jamaicans, however. In my searches through records I have found items which might be of interest to American as well as British researchers. For example, a marriage reported to take place in 1793 in Hampshire, England, actually took place in St. Catherine's Parish, Jamaica, after which the person moved to England and died in Southampton, hence the guesstimate that the marriage also took place in England. Some marriages of men who served in the regiments sent from England to Jamaica are recorded in Jamaica, and first and second born children may be christened in Jamaica. English and American ships captains, mates and ordinary seamen may be buried in Jamaica, although they truly never lived in the island. English Quakers who settled in the island in the late 17th century removed to Pennsylvania in the 18th century. American Loyalists who fled to Jamaica after the American Revolution may have filtered back to the United States or joined others in Canada. Germans who first immigrated to Jamaica later settled after the 1850s in the American Midwest.

Many midwestern and western Americans have traced their families back to the United States East Coast and deduced that they originated in the United Kingdom in the 1600-1750 period, but they can not find where the immigrant ancestor came from. Many know about Barbados, St. Kitts and Nevis as a possible way-stop before reaching America, but few seem to have considered Jamaica as an equally likely island for searching. A fellow researcher at my local Family History Center of the Mormon Church (Moscow, Idaho) was delighted when I showed him that his family surname existed in Jamaica in about 1705, because he had "lost" the family in North Carolina in about 1740. Many families of the surname existed in England but he had been unable to make any connections to his family. He is now busily searching Jamaican records.

In the early period of North America, people traveled much more extensively between the West Indies and the East Coast of the United States than I had realized. For example, a 1674 will of a relative who died in Boston, Mass., named as the executor his son-in-law, who was at that time a planter in Jamaica. The testator fully expected that this executor would come to Boston to tidy up his affairs, but made contingency plans for his wife's protection if the said executor was not able to get to Boston immediately. The will was probated and cleared within the year by the executor. So, North Americans, don't overlook Jamaica if you have "lost" records of an immigrant ancestor!

I remember the instructor of the first course I took on genealogy warning about offense you can cause by digging up family history that others would rather keep secret and how "kept secrets" can sometimes lead the researcher astray. The examples given were things such as prison records, the horse thief and the highwayman. In Jamaica, the areas most likely to give problems are illegitimacy and colour. In Jamaica today, the illegitimacy rate can be as high as 70%. In the climate of the end of the 20th century, illegitimacy may not seem like a big deal, with movie stars and other entertainers having children out of wedlock and the prevalence of teenage out-of-wedlock births, but in the early part of the century and the Victorian era many out-of-wedlock births were covered up by the family. My mother says that it was not unheard of in her mother's generation for a younger sister to go and stay to help out an older sister during the birth of particularly her first child. Nine months after the beginning of the visit, the younger sister would have a child by the older sister's husband. The fact was well known, but not spoken about outside the inner family. You may find the record documents, however, quite accurate. This can disconcert the older generation when you record that a male relative had two families, one of which was not by a verified wife.

Colour or race is even more likely to be covered up, especially if the family ever "passed for white" or if for some reason the family did not want it known that the father of a child was East Indian, or white. Actually since we are "Out of Many, one People" (The Jamaican Motto) very few Jamaican families who lived in the island for three or more generations are pure of any race, Black, White, Chinese or Syrian etc. I think you will have most difficulty with those older relatives who were never told the reality, so do not want to hear it now. You can handle it by saying that what matters is what people were and did in their lives not the circumstances of how they were born.

My thanks are due to the many librarians, archivists and researchers who have helped me. And special appreciation is extended to my second and third cousins who have made trips to Jamaica and brought me back many materials. The errors in this book, however, are all mine. If I had been researching for 30 years maybe there would not be any errors, but it has been just 13 years since I began detailed study. I welcome corrections and additions to this manuscript.

I am assuming that the user of this book has some knowledge of how to go about researching family history, e.g. pedigrees, family group sheets and research documentation, etc. If not, the place to begin is at your local library where there are usually many books to help you get started. I first used *Ancestry's Guide to Research: Case Studies in American Genealogy* by Johni Cerny and Arlene Eakle, published by Ancestry Incorporated, Salt Lake City, Utah, 1985 (ISBN 0-916489-01-9) and also *Discovering your Family History* by Don Steel, edited by Bryn Brooks, published by the British Broadcasting Corporation, 1980 (ISBN 0-563-16286-4); but there are many others to choose from which are just as good.

Madeleine E. Mitchell
NE 1010 Alfred Lane
Pullman, WA 99163
December 26, 1997

Abbreviations

ARCH ....Archives of Jamaica, Spanish Town

FHL...........Family History Library, Genealogical Society of Utah, Salt Lake City, Utah

IGI.............International Genealogical Index (LDS)

IJ ....Institute of Jamaica, now National Library

IREC ....Island Record Office, Spanish Town, now the Registrar General's Office (RGO), Twickenham Park, Spanish Town

ISBN ....International Standard Book Number

LDS...........Latter-day Saints, Mormon Church

NA...........National Archives, Kew, London formerly the Public Record Office

NLJ ....National Library of Jamaica, formerly the Institute of Jamaica, Kingston (IJ)

PRO ....Public Record Office, Kew, London now the National Archives

RCS...........Royal Commonwealth Society Library, Cambridge, England

RGO..........Registrar General's Office, formerly Island Record Office (IREC), Twickenham Park, Spanish Town

SoG...........Society of Genealogy, London

Introduction

The golden rule of good genealogy is to go from the known backwards to the unknown, so first you will want to gather all the information you can from near relatives and friends. If your family immigrated to North America or England in the last half of the 20th century, they probably had to have certified copies of birth and marriage certificates for passports, and of course immigration visas and naturalization papers. Knowing the **parish** in Jamaica from which your family came should be a goal of examining these papers. (For more about parishes see the chapter on Maps.) It is vital that you know the parish because many of the sources that are listed or discussed in this book are listed by **parish** in the depositories. This is similar in the UK of knowing the county and in the US of knowing the state.

Oral History

If you cannot find the basic information about your mother and father's birthplace, then talk to relatives. I have always counted myself lucky for living in a small island. I knew my second and third cousins and their families, not just my first cousins and nuclear family. This led to a family Bible coming to my attention from a third cousin. Family Bibles often recorded births, marriages and deaths. Other records that cousins may have include birthday books, autograph albums, and photograph albums, deeds and wills. A checklist for Family and Home information sources (geared to North America but useful elsewhere) is at:http://www.pbs.org/kbyu/ancestors/teachersguide/tg-images/housform.gif. And listen to the stories about the families. Sometimes the oral tradition that has been passed down in the family as to where the first immigrant to Jamaica came from may be the only clue on where to start looking in the old countries. Sometimes you will of course get conflicting information, and sometimes it will be totally in error, but that is better than nothing at all. One branch of my family maintains that an ancestor came from Germany while another cousin says she heard the family came from Somerset, England. I have not found him yet, but I am looking.

If you have no aunts, uncles, cousins or grandparents living in your neighbourhood (or do not have their addresses), talk to those Jamaicans of their generation who do. Even though they are not family, the older generation might have an amazing amount of knowledge about your family. Remember it is a small island; news traveled rapidly. A lot of gossip was about families. Someone may have a cousin whose aunt was a bridesmaid in a wedding you are interested in. Someone's grandmother may have been a midwife in the district. An acquaintance's uncle could have been a lawyer, and could know something about the family you are interested in.

There are several computer programs for entering your data and keeping track of what you have found. A commercial program very popular with genealogists is Family Tree Maker. http://familytreemaker.genealogy.com/ A free program is put out by the Family History Library called Personal Ancestral File (PAF) at: http://www.familysearch.org/. (Find Order/Download Products then find Software Downloads free at the next page).

When you have gathered all your oral history and drafted your first pedigrees and family group sheets, you may wish to start at the chapter on Civil Registrations or the chapter on Vital and Church Records depending on the dates for which you are searching.

A Short List of Events in Jamaica

1494 Jamaica discovered by Christopher Columbus
1655 British conquer Jamaica, driving out Spanish
1692 Earthquake, destroys Port Royal
1739 End of the first Maroon War
1796 End of the second Maroon War
1807 Slave trade with West Africa abolished
1834 Abolition of Slavery
1838 Apprenticeship abolished
1865 Morant Bay Rebellion
1938 Trade Unions established
1962 Independence from Britain, Member of the Commonwealth

For a more detailed list of events, see the Appendix.

Civil Registration

Most of your work on family history records will begin with this section, after you compile pedigrees or family group sheets. This is true if you are working backwards from the known to the unknown (recommended).

Registration of births, deaths and marriages by the government, otherwise known as Civil Registration, was started in approximately 1880 in Jamaica and continues to the present day. This contrasts to Civil Registration in England which began in 1837. Thus for Jamaica a greater part of the nineteenth century records are found in church records 1800-1880 rather than the records of the government, 1880-1900. Records for the twentieth century are found in Civil Registration, 1900 to the present.

Registrars were appointed in districts within each parish and people were required to register the vital events with them. Sometimes a clergyman was appointed a marriage officer and sent a duplicate registration of the marriage to the registrar. The records of the individual registrars were sent in to Spanish Town, where they are now kept in the Registrar General's Office. The Church of Jesus Christ of Latter-day Saints (the Mormons) has filmed the Civil Registration records from 1880 to 1990's, and the indexes to some of these records from 1880 to approximately 1930. They are available at the FHLibrary at Salt Lake City, Utah http://www.familysearch.org, and in Family History Centers all over the world. (Look in your telephone book for an LDS church and telephone to find the location and hours of operation of the center nearest to you. Or on the Family History site: http://www.familysearch.org/Eng/Library/FHC/frameset_fhc.asp it will help you find a Family History Center world wide.)

The precise dates of indexes and registrations vary by parish.

Parish	Births	Deaths	Marriages
St Ann	1878-1930	1878-1995	1880-1950
St Mary	1878-1930	1878-1994	1880-1950
Portland	1878-1930	1878-1995	1880-1950
St Thomas	1878-1930	1878-1995	1880-1950
Kingston	1878-1927	1878-1995	1880-1950
St Andrew	1878-1930	1878-1995	1880-1950
St Catherine	1878-1930	1871-1995	1880-1950
Clarendon	1878-1930	1878-1995	1880-1950
Manchester	1878-1930	1878-1992	1885-1950
St Elizabeth	1878-1930	1878-1995	1880-1950
Westmoreland	1878-1930	1878-1995	1880-1950
Hanover	1878-1930	1878-1995	1884-1950
St James	1878-1930	1883-1995	1880-1950
Trelawny	1878-1930	1878-1995	1880-1950
Jamaica Civil Registration, St Catherine, St Andrew, St Thomas and Kingston	Miscellaneous Births 1924-1930		

Thus the Civil Registration records of Jamaica are available through Family History Centers for a small fee and copies of events can be obtained from Salt Lake City for a copying fee or they may be copied at a Center on a microfilm copier. (At Spanish Town, the services of providing copies of Civil Registrations are overwhelmed with requests since the government requires all school children to present registered birth certificates to attend school. It can take a whole day, sometimes more, to obtain one vital certificate. In fact the latest information given to me is that family history seekers may only access these records on Thursdays.

You can obtain certified copies of birth, death and marriage certificates on-line from the Registrar General's Department http://www.rgd.gov.jm/ (.I have had a varied response from people who have gone this route. Some obtained certificates rapidly, others waited months or over a year). A certified copy is not a requirement for genealogical purposes, thus it is faster and more efficient to find your records through the films available at a Family History Center. Register films and a reader are also available in the Family History Center of the

LDS church in Gore Terrace, St. Andrew, but I am not sure that the reader can read the high reduction films of the indexes.

Indexes

Surname indexes to deaths and marriages may be found in the FHL Catalog under Jamaica/Civil Registration/Indexes. As of April 2005, birth indexes were not yet available for most parishes, but are available for St Elizabeth in some cases 1878-1919.with some gaps. Some CD-ROMs of the FHL Catalog do not have Civil Registration indexes under Jamaica/, so check under Jamaica/Parish/Civil Registration on the CD — this is the latest manner of indexing the civil registrations. Alternately, check the microfiche copy of the catalog.   Each parish is given a letter code:

          A – Kingston
          B – St. Andrew
          C – St. Thomas
          D – Portland
          E – St. Catherine
          F – St. Mary
          G – St. Ann
          H – Clarendon
          I – Manchester
          K – St. Elizabeth
          L – Westmoreland
          M – Hanover
          N – St. James
          O – Trelawny
          P – Cayman Island

Thus you need to know the parish and approximate date of the event, but this is a great deal easier than before the indexes were available.

Indexes	Births	Deaths	Marriages
Indexes to Most parishes	1878-1879 1884-1885	1878-1930	1871-1930
Clarendon, Manchester and St Elizabeth	1890,1894		
St Elizabeth	1878-1919 with gaps		
Cayman		1878-1930	1871-1930

Death indexes actually begin in 1878, and the years 1878-1887 are found on one film (10 items) for all parishes. Thus to search the whole period 1878 to 1930 on the indexes you need to look at nine high reduction (42x) 16 mm films. A few volumes are missing.

The marriage indexes actually begin in 1871 and are for Church of England marriages for 1871-1879 (one film, one item). Beginning in 1880 brides' and bridegrooms' surnames are listed in separate volumes, up to 1902; and beginning in 1903 the names of the parties are listed in the same volume, up to 1930. This index is made up of eight high reduction (42x) 16 mm films.

Birth indexes as of 2005 have not been listed on the online catalog site except for a few years shown above and in the film notes. They state that the index for 1880 for all parishes is missing.. The indexes for birth concentrate primarily on St Elizabeth with some for Clarendon and Manchester. Indexes for 1914, 1915, 1917, 1918 and 1920 are missing. There are two high resolution series films for these indexes.

Registrations

The registrar recorded the event on wide preprinted forms and each form has been filmed separately, and is filed by district (FHL Catalog: Jamaica/Civil Registration or Jamaica/Parish/Civil Registration). The catalog lists the films by year and by parish. No districts are given for each film in the catalog, but all the districts for each parish are listed in the Film notes heading. There are numbers stamped and written on each record which overlap with those of other districts within the same parish, so be sure you have found the right district within a parish before concluding that the index is wrong.

Births

The following items will generally be found on a birth certificate. (Example 1910)

Heading: Birth in the District of _____ Parish of _____

Date and Place of Birth
Name (if any)
Sex
Name and Surname and Dwelling-place of Father
Name and Surname and Maiden Surname of Mother
Rank or Profession of Father

Signature, Qualification and Residence of Informant
When Registered
Baptismal Name if added after Registration

Footer: Signature of Informant. Name of Registrar.
    District Parish

An abbreviated square copy of this registration containing the name of the child and date was given to the parents in later years, but it was not considered a certified copy if, for example, you wished to obtain a passport.

Marriages
The following items would be expected on a marriage registration. (Example 1893)

Heading: Marriage Register

Number
When Married
Name and Surname of Parties
Condition (e.g. Widower, Spinster)
Calling (Occupation)
Age (Years)
Parish and Residence at the Time of Marriage
Father's Name and Surname of Each Party

Footer: Married at _____ by or before me _____, a
    Marriage Officer of the Parish of _____

This Marriage was celebrated between us _____
    (Signatures of each party) in the presence of us
    _____ (Signatures of two witnesses)

Deaths
The following items would be expected on the death registration. (Example 1899)

Header: Death in the District of _____ Parish of _____

Date and Place of Death
Name and Surname
Sex
Condition (Married, Single)
Age Last Birthday
Rank, Profession or Occupation
Certified Cause of Death and Duration of Illness (Name
    of Certifier)
Signature, Qualification and Residence of Informer
When Registered

Footer: Signed by the said (informant) in the presence of
_____ Registrar of Births and Deaths _____
District, Parish of _____

I assume that there were some changes over the years, but I have not examined enough of them to discern where the changes may be. One of the bonuses of getting a marriage registration as opposed to a church record of this time is that you can see the actual signature (or mark, usually a cross if the person could not write) of your ancestor. If one of the informants on a birth or death certificate or the witnesses to the marriage was a relative, you will also have additional names of people alive at that time, but the informants' signatures are not originals, whereas the witnesses to a marriage are original signatures.

What do you gain from getting copies of these events? Well for a marriage you get the names of the fathers of the bride and groom thus going back one generation. You often get an age so that you can estimate the year of birth of the bride and groom respectively. Even if you already know this information it is good to have this as documentation. For birth certificates you will often get the maiden name of the mother as well as the occupation of the father. These clues are very helpful in going further back in time. Do not overlook witnesses and informants as these can be living relatives.

Civil Registration in England , Wales and Scotland

I am not attempting to cover this topic comprehensively here. I recommend that if you need to use the records covered in the next two sections in this chapter that you obtain books and other aids to research which review this material in depth.

Civil Registration began in 1837 in England and Wales, and in Scotland in 1855 thus if your ancestors went to the UK you may want to look for their births, deaths or marriages in the records there before you get back to Church records or Civil registration in Jamaica.

The records for England and Wales are held in the Family Records Centre, 1 Myddelton Street, London EC1R 1UW Here you can search their indexes and order certificates. Some of these indexes are available also in County Record Offices as microfiche. The SoG has a copy. The records for Scotland are held at the General Register Office of Scotland, New Regisiter House, 3 West Register Street, Edinburgh EH1 3YT. The latters indexes can be searched for a fee at the Family Records Centre, London or online for a fee.

There are several online sources for these records some of which charge fees.

For England and Wales there is Free BMD at http://freebmd.rootsweb.com/ cgi/search.pl This is not yet complete (1837 up to 1910 in 2005) and you can check on the homepage to find out if the year you are interested has been covered. The advantage is it is free. For a fee you can use http://www.1837online.com (1837-2003 in 2005) These both are indexes and give the quarter in the year of interest,. volumes and page numbers of the pertinent records. To get the certificates on line you can order at http://www.gro.gov.uk/gro/content/certificate/index.asp#0. You do need the quarter of the year, the volume and page in order to order the certificates with a credit card online or in person at the Family Records center.

For Scotland the relevant URL is http://www.scotlandspeople.gov.uk/. Indexes to Scottish civil registers for: births over 100 years old; marriages over 75 years old; and deaths over 50 years old are available here. In 2005 it costs £6 to search for 30 page credits valid for 168 consecutive hours. For an additional fee you can obtain the certificate.

Civil Registration/Vital Records in Canada and the United States

In Canada the **provinces** and territories have the responsibility of recording Civil Registration. A site which gives the links to the provinces and tells the date of birth,death and marriage records available is: http://www.genealogy.gc.ca/10/100606_e.html. Some of the Provincial archives have on-line databases which can be searched.

In the United States birth death and marriage information is only available by **state**. An online starting point to write for vital records is: http://www.cdc.gov/nchs/howto/w2w/w2welcom.htm. The

USGenWeb Project http://www.rootsweb.com/~usgw/ also leads to online records. If you do not know what state to look in two sources are helpful, the US Censuses (up to 1930) and the Social Security Death Index (SSDI). Both are available for a fee at http://ancestry.com/. Also helpful if your ancestor entered the US via New York in the 1892-1924 period is the Ellis Island Records at: http://www.ellisislandrecords.org/ Often the record shows at least an initial destination. This site is free.

Church Records

If you have traced your genealogy back to before 1878-1880 in Jamaica by using Civil Registration records from Jamaica, England or Canada you will want to move backwards to Church records to further your research.

Remember that many of the records covered in this section will really be christenings or baptisms and burials, because they are derived from church records which were chiefly concerned with the ceremonies of the church. Civil Registration Records listed actual birth and death dates.

IGI – International Genealogical Index

As a finding source, the International Genealogical Index (IGI), previously called the CFI (Computer File Index), of the Church of Jesus Christ of Latter-day Saints (usually called LDS or the Mormons) is a great boon to those who do not know the county or parish origin of their forebears in countries worldwide (but heavily weighted to the United Kingdom and the U.S. and Canada). It is available at the FHLibrary at Salt Lake City, Utah http://www.familysearch.org, and in Family History Centers all over the world. (Look in your telephone book for an LDS church and telephone to find the location and hours of operation of the center nearest to you. Or on the Family History site: http://www.familysearch.org/Eng/Library/FHC/frameset_fhc.asp will help you find a Family History Center world wide.) The format may either be microfiche or, more recently, computer CD-ROM. The IGI is also available on line at: <http://www.familysearch.org/Eng/Search/ frameset_search.asp?PAGE=igi/search_IGI.asp&clear_form=true>. In England there is a center in London, and the Genealogical Society in

Goswell Road has a copy of the IGI in Microfiche. The Guildhall Library in London also holds a microfilm and a microfiche copy. (County libraries in England hold fiche for their county but not in general for the whole world.)

There is a section of the IGI for the West Indies, but Jamaican searchers will be disappointed. The majority of entries in the 1997 edition (Version 4.00) of the IGI for the West Indies have been extracted from Barbados. The few records from Jamaica which are included are from LDS member submissions prior to 1970 and as I said are very small in number. Still it is worth a quick review, especially if the IGI you encounter is on the CD-ROM or computer search system. My understanding is that some members of the church are engaged as part of their obligations in extraction of the Jamaican records but not at many locations, so it is not known when the IGI will be very much further advanced in Jamaican records. If you find little to help, this should not deter you from starting your research; there are other avenues.

In the current edition of the IGI, over 200 million names of persons in the world have been computerized, chiefly consisting of christening, baptismal and marriage records listed by county. There are very few burial or death records because members of the church do not need such records to perform temple ordinances. Remember that if you do find an entry in the IGI this is not proof of the event. Errors (names spelled incorrectly for example) might have occurred in extraction so you should always seek verification in the original documents from which the extraction was made. Sources are indicated in the IGI; write them down for further reference. In addition, the original source may contain more information which may be valuable in your research. For example, a christening may include the names of godfathers and godmothers who may or may not be related; marriages may include witnesses.

A trap that the beginner can fall into is that having found a person in the IGI with a surname identical to the one for which he is searching, the researcher assumes that he or she MUST be related and spends a great deal of time following up this lead, when no connection has been made to the presently known family branches. By all means if the surname is unusual, especially in a small island like Jamaica, make a note of the reference for later searches, but work backwards from the known to the unknown before spending a great deal of time following up unconnected but name-related leads found in the IGI. For example, if you have traced back to 1890 in a family line and find a person of the surname in the IGI in 1745, it is more profitable in the long run to continue tracing back from 1890 than to trace forward from 1745. They may never connect!

Another searching aid in the Family History Centers with computer capabilities is the AF or Ancestry File. The LDS church is encouraging members and non-members to contribute their family research in GEDCOM format (a standardized computer genealogical format) to this computer file which is periodically put out on CD-ROM. I have not found it very useful for Jamaican families, but if your family has been in North America for a generation or two you may find information of use. Also available fairly recently, at Family History Centers and commercially, on CD-ROM is the United States Social Security Death Index, which can be a very good starting place if your ancestor worked and died in the United States since 1935. The index leads you to the date and place of death, information necessary to access further records in the Social Security Administration which can give you the date and place of birth. Ask about how to do this at the Family History Center; the volunteers are very helpful.

Church of England (Anglican, Episcopalian)

The established church of Jamaica after Columbus discovered the island was Roman Catholicism (see Roman Catholics, below). After the conquest by England in 1655, the established church was the Church of England (Anglican, Episcopalian). From 1655 to 1824 the established churches in Jamaica were under the jurisdiction of the Bishop of London, after which a diocese was established and a Bishop of Jamaica was named. These church archives are the source of vital records from the 1600s up to 1880, when Civil Registration began. Each **parish** kept its own christening, marriage and burial records and these records are deposited in the Island Record Office, now the Registrar General's Office in Spanish Town, Jamaica. This is why it is important to know the **parish** of origin.

Parishes
(See also Maps)

Jamaica was divided into three counties, Surrey, Middlesex and Cornwall, but church records were kept by parish not county. There were as many as 22 parishes in 1844 compared to the present 14 parishes. Therefore if you do not have a location which can be identified within a parish it will be difficult but not impossible to find church records. To summarize the parishes and changes I will divide them into Original Parishes and Changed Parishes.

Original Parishes

Original Parishes include: St Ann, St Mary, St George, St Thomas in the East (now St Thomas), St Andrew, Port Royal, St David, St Catherine, St John, Clarendon, St Elizabeth, St James.

Changed parishes

Changed parishes include:

Metcalfe, created from St George and St Mary in 1841 and absorbed by St Mary 1866;

Portland, created from St George and St Thomas in the East 1723;

St Thomas in the East a portion of which was absorbed by Portland, 1866;

St David, absorbed by St Thomas in the East, 1866

Port Royal, of which a portion was absorbed by Kingston and the rest by St Andrew, 1866;

Kingston which separated from St Andrew, 1693

St Dorothy was separated from Clarendon, 1675 and absorbed by St Catherine 1866;

St John was absorbed by St Catherine 1866;

Vere was separated from Clarendon in 1673 and reabsorbed by the same in 1866;

St Thomas in the Vale was separated from St Catherine in 1675 and reabsorbed by the same in 1866;

Manchester was created from Vere, Clarendon and St Elizabeth in 1814

Westmoreland was split off from St Elizabeth, 1703;

Hanover was separated from Westmoreland in 1723

Trelawny was split off from St James in 1770.

Present Parishes

The current parishes since 1866 for church records and those also current for Civil Registration include: St Ann, St Mary, Portland, St Thomas, Kingston, St Andrew, St Catherine, Clarendon, Manchester, St Elizabeth, Westmoreland, Hanover, St James and Trelawny.

Parish Records
Spanish Town, Jamaica

The parish records have been filmed by the Church of Jesus Christ of Latter-day Saints (Mormons). Copies of the films are held by the General Registrar's Office at Twickenham Park or the National Archives in Spanish Town and may be read on microfilm reader and copies made. This is more convenient and puts less strain on the original documents. (See below for more information.)

FHLibrary – Genealogical Society of Utah

As mentioned above, the Anglican church records of Jamaica have been filmed by the LDS church (Mormons) and therefore are available not only in Salt Lake City, but in Family History Centers throughout North America, Australia, England and Jamaica (see IGI section for finding a family history center). The catalog of the FHLibrary (on microfiche or CD-ROM) can be consulted to find the number of the film (FHL Catalog: Jamaica/Church Records) and then films may be ordered for a nominal fee for 30 days, or slightly more for 60 days.

Alternatively you can find the film number from the FHL catalog on line at: http://www.familysearch.org/Eng/Library/FHLC/frameset_fhlc.asp (After you reach this home page you will put in a place name search for Jamaica and search on Jamaica church records, then parish register transcripts 1664-1880.) Then armed with this information you can order the films in your local Family History center. Some Family History Centers have microfilm readers/copiers; others just have microfilm and fiche readers. If the latter, after you identify the page you can fill out a form (available in the center) and send to Salt Lake City for a copy for a copying fee. If the center has a reader/copier you can have copies made on the spot.

The section on church records of Jamaica in the FHL Catalog has a long introduction, explaining (1) the record series and (2) the original parishes, and the changes in the parishes. Read this section carefully, and if the catalog is on CD-ROM print out the record for reference. Another source of FHCenter film numbers on the web is: http://www.candoo.com/genresources/jamaica.htm#DOJR, but I have not used it so cannot verify its completeness or accuracy. Yet third source is Patricia Jackson's website Jamaican Family search at: http://jamaicanfamilysearch.com/Samples/fhclist.htm which covers the parish registers from 1664-1880. This site has many free pages but also has members pages for a modest fee. For example in 2006 it costs $8.00 for a month, $70.00 for a year to join. This free page which lists Family History Center films is excellent because it lists corrections to the Family History Center catalog in red. A printout of this page is about 18 pages of American letter size paper.

Indexes

There is no all-island name index, but each parish has an index film, which may contain up to four alphabetical name index volumes taking you up to 1872 and what are called Law 6 registers. Each index volume is divided into baptisms, marriages and burials. Baptisms or christenings are the largest section. Under each letter of the alphabet the names are arranged chronologically, not strictly alphabetically; therefore you will need to search several pages, especially in the first index volume. By the second and third index volume, the names under each letter of the alphabet are divided by year or by a short year span, e.g. 1860-62. Some indexes have been lost over the years, e.g. the first index volume for St. Ann (noted in the catalog). It is important for finding the event that you carefully note the volume and page or folio from the index. Sometimes the ink is smeared or the index volume is bound too tightly to see the page number. Read the records before and after the record of interest and read the column heading. Often the transcriber used ditto marks down the entire column. Take particular care after 1825, when the index to the volumes of records were recorded as Volume 1 "new series", or Volume 1— two entirely different registers and films.

There are separate indexes for 1860-71 for baptisms, marriages and burials. They are listed in the FHL Catalog under Parish Registers, Miscellaneous Baptism Index, Miscellaneous Marriage Index and Miscellaneous Burial Index. These indexes are incomplete and overlap with some of the parish indexes above.

In 1871 Law 6 was enacted, and there are Law 6 indexes for baptisms, marriages and burials. These cover the period 1870 to 1880 when Civil Registration began. There is overlap on both ends of the time period with respect to these indexes and to the registers.

Registers

The registers of events are fairly straightforward for the first series, i.e. from the beginning of the record to 1825. Each parish has its own register. The earliest registers begin in 1666, e.g. St. Andrew and Clarendon; others begin as late as 1804, e.g. Portland. Some early St. James records are found in the Hanover register. Sometimes in the earliest entries to registers, christenings, marriages and burials are on the same page, but that only occurs some of the time and not for very long.

Some registers have only five or so entries for the date at which the film begins and then entries jump forward 30 or so years.

After 1824, when the diocese was established, the records become more complicated. The Stipendiary Curates and Island Curates who traveled to the consecrated chapels in a parish sent returns to the rector of the parish in the capital town, who periodically (it was supposed to be annually, then quarterly) sent his and others returns to the Diocesan Registry Office in Spanish Town, where a clerk entered them into register books. Later there were different volumes for christenings, marriages and burials. Thus four to five parishes' christenings or marriages or burials will be in one register. However, they are not always separated into four or five sections of the book, but were recorded as they came in. Each register of this series has on the first page a list of the parishes included and the pages on which entries start being recorded for each parish. In a single volume the starting date for marriages, burials or christenings may be different by parish because some parishes were sparsely populated and entries were made until they filled up the space allotted and then were carried forward to other volumes. In later volumes of this series, lists for quarterly returns for up to 10 parishes may be in one volume, as they came into the diocesan office. This is why it is best to read the parish indexes first, even if you know the date of the event; otherwise you may find yourself ordering many films in order to find the correct entry.

Beginning in 1815 but particularly at the abolition of slavery, 1834, the Anglican church began records of christening, marriages and burials of slaves or former slaves in large numbers. Sometimes these were kept in separate volumes (e.g. Hanover), sometimes in the back of a current volume. The LDS film catalog does not usually identify these records separately, but Ingram in *Sources of Jamaican History* (see History References) has a list that denotes by parish when slave records began.

In 1837 in England, Civil Registration was started, and in 1844 an attempt was made to do the same in Jamaica; however, the law was largely ignored and was repealed in 1851. Thus this period is not referred to as Civil Registration in Jamaica. Records were supposed to be sent in to a registrar in Spanish Town, where preprinted pages of the register were filled in. This series, 1844-51, has births and deaths recorded as opposed to christenings and burials. Since at this time there were a number of non-conformist churches operating, these registers do contain dissenting entries. However they are not exclusively dissenting registers, which can be verified by noting the name of the officiating minister and comparing it to the name of Anglican ministers in the appropriate parish.

I had an experience with registers labeled Dissenter Marriages that I wish to warn about. I had found a marriage citation in the index for St. Ann in which the volume and page number were very clear. I tried several films which should have contained the referred-to marriage, no luck. Finally, when I was in Salt Lake City, in desperation I tried the films labeled Dissenter Marriages although I knew the family was Anglican. I did find it in such a volume. It was a record sent in by the curate for St. Mark's Chapel, Brown's Town, an Anglican Chapel. In the same volume were records from St. John's and St. Luke's Chapels. These are all Anglican chapels in St. Ann. I think what happened is that later in the nineteenth century, someone in charge of rebinding the registers found these records from chapels and thought they referred to non-conformist chapels, so labeled them Dissenter Marriages. The rest of the register is indeed non-conformist marriages, usually with the name of the denomination of the minister e.g. Baptist, Methodist. Records of non-conformists are very distinctive in format giving 2-3 inches with headings per record, while the Anglican chapel records have one heading per page with a line or two for each record. My advice is, therefore, if you cannot find an indexed Anglican marriage record, try the Dissenter Marriage registers.

To summarize, the films of registers prior to 1825 and after 1870 (Law 6 registers) are relatively easy to use. The period between 1826 and 1869 can be very confusing, because of overlapping dates.

Notes on Registers

• 1. It must be obvious from the above discussion that there was extensive copying of the entries even in registers thought to be original, prior to 1825. For example, in St. Catherine's Parish, in one of the oldest registers, in 1775 there is a paragraph verifying that the current rector had made a true copy of the former registers. This is borne out in the baptismal section of the first volume, where the entries are in double columns, all in the same uniform hand writing, year after year. This was not how any other original register was handled. Westmoreland was split off from St. Elizabeth in 1703, but no vital events are recorded in the parish register prior to 1739. Westmoreland suffered from severe hurricanes four years in a row in the 1780s and I suspect that only some fragments remained from the early original books which were copied into what is now Westmoreland, Volume 1, to 1825. It is my opinion that original entries are most likely to exist between 1780 and 1825. After 1825, we have essentially bishops' transcripts which were copied at least once, if not three times (curate to rector, rector to diocesan office, diocesan clerk to register). The more times the event was copied, the more likely for errors to creep in.

• 2. The early clergy were very blunt about colour. (After the abolition of slavery, colour was often encoded in the rank or profession column; see Note 4.) Thus you see entries such as:

> Mary Green, a free black baptized 22 September 1780

or

> John Clark, a free mulatto man and Jane, a sambo slave
> were married 22nd August 1801.

These designations can tell you how many generations back a white or black ancestor was in the family line, because there was a convention in designating colour that the English assumed from the Spanish. This convention was:

> The offspring of a white and a black was a mulatto.
> The offspring of a white and a mulatto was a quadroon.
> The offspring of a white and a quadroon was a mustee
> (mestee), mustifino (very rarely an octoroon).
> The offspring of a white and a mustee was white, by law.
> The offspring of a mulatto and a black was a sambo.
> The offspring of a sambo and a black was black.

Other designations besides the above and African, black or white were used, but these are less descriptive of lineage. They include: "Of Colour" and "Brown" (which could mean sambo, mulatto, quadroon or mustee). One inventive minister used the rich-sounding term "Sable". Except for the offspring of a white and a mustee, any people designated as listed above could be slaves; having some white ancestry did not convey freedom, although these persons were more likely to be baptized than Africans. Look for the term "free" or "free person of colour" or "free African" to designate people who had gained their freedom. It follows that the term "slave" used for a person in the record, while most likely to be designated black, might have had white ancestry. In the parish register of Westmoreland between 1780 and 1814, the pages were divided into White Persons and Non-White Persons, but this is the only register in which I have seen this colour division.

"Creole" is a misunderstood term, perhaps because it changed in meaning over the years. Originally "Creole" simply meant born in the island as opposed to being born in Britain or Africa. So there were Creole whites and Creole blacks. Among negro slave names, Creole Jack was born in Jamaica, but African Jack was born in Africa. Lady Nugent in her remarks in 1803 about some of the white Creole women that she met was very scathing about their drawling speech and manners; she obviously considered them inferior to persons educated and socialized in England. She called women she met of mixed parentage, brown ladies. By the end of the nineteenth century, "Creole" was usually used to denote someone of mixed parentage, born in the island. There does not seem to be a particular period in which this occurred, so care should be used in interpretation of this term.

• 3. Many white men claimed their mulatto, quadroon and mustee children and gave them their surnames; however, there are ample examples where the paternity was in doubt, in which case you will see "reputed son of" etc. Unlike early English parish records, I have never come across the term "base child of" or "bastard daughter of". If no parents are listed or if only the mother is listed, the child is most likely to be illegitimate; however, keep in mind the copying errors, including omissions, that could have occurred. In Port Royal registers, for one clergyman's records, both the parents are named, e.g. "John Grey and Mary Murray, parents of George Grey", and a column designates whether they were married or not married. In this case, you cannot assume that because Mary's maiden name is given rather than "wife of" that they were not married. However, in most other cases in which the mother's maiden name is given, it is most likely that the parents were not married.

• 4. Other terminology that is used in the vital records refers to the profession, rank or occupation of the father, which entered the records routinely after 1834. The hierarchy of the plantation was represented, namely:

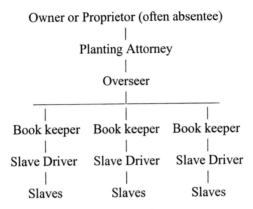

Owner or Proprietor (often absentee)
|
Planting Attorney
|
Overseer

Book keeper	Book keeper	Book keeper
Slave Driver	Slave Driver	Slave Driver
Slaves	Slaves	Slaves

All those above Slave Driver were white. Slave drivers and slaves were black or of colour and in the new designation of 1834 were "apprentices". After 1838 they were called "labourers". The "Planting Attorney" usually had responsibilities for more than one estate. The euphemism for proprietor, book keeper and overseer was "planter" up to about the 1870s, when non-conformist ministers began applying it to any who worked in agriculture. "Book keepers" did not usually keep books: they were out in the fields supervising the slave gangs. "Small settler" at first was applied to white immigrants who came out to Jamaica in the 1840s, mostly German, with the promise of land. After Civil Registration in 1880 this term was used for anyone working small pieces of the land. On the plantations, prior to emancipation, the most valuable slaves were those with professions such as masons, carpenters and coopers. These continued to be professional designations for former slaves, during apprenticeship and after 1838. Practitioners of Physic (Doctors), Lawyers (Attorneys), Schoolmasters, Anglican Clergy, Policemen and Customs Officers were generally white up to 1900. During the same time frame, someone with the profession Shopkeeper was generally a converted Jew, or of mixed parentage; a Merchant was white.

• 5. The number of entries in the parish registers fell sharply between 1826 and 1834. I am not sure of the reason for this, but there must have been some confusion at the changeover from the Bishop of London to the Bishop of Jamaica in how the latter wanted records handled. Also, in 1831-32 there was a slave rebellion in St. James and Trelawny, and perhaps the curates were not riding the circuits, especially in the interior parts of the island. Possibly some of the non-conformist churches were making inroads into the Anglican congregations, especially among new working-class whites not in the capital of the parish, who were recruited to balance the number of blacks. The Anglican clergy supporting the planters in the debate over abolition of slavery alienated the free coloured people, who turned to the Methodists and Baptists. It is also true that sugar production peaked in about 1805 and the estates, anticipating the end of slavery, began to lose white book keepers and overseers who sold out and left the island. Beginning in 1834, there was a great increase in the records as the clergy went from estate to estate marrying and baptizing former slaves, sometimes as many as 100 in one day.

• 6. Burials are fewer in number in the records, except for the capital town of the parish. This makes sense, because there was no way in the tropics for preserving the body and burial occurred either on the same day or the day after death. If a curate was not within riding distance, the burial might not have been recorded, especially those which occurred on estates. When a burial did occur, you can usually assume that the date of death was within one day, even if date of death is not recorded. Prior to 1825, there are a number of burials recorded in Spanish Town, of people who lived in other parishes. I suspect that they died in the capital while on business and it was judged too hard to get them home for burial. Christenings in the capital of each parish were probably within a month of birth, but this is a risky assumption out of the chief town. In the early records you may notice several children being christened together. I noticed particularly if there were two girls and then a boy, the parents waited until the boy was born and then had them all christened. It was probably for convenience of the minister and because of the cost of having him come out to the country parts. I have also noticed a number of times, where a man had illegitimate children, he would have all the children he had by the woman baptized just around and before the time he got married, usually to a different woman.

• 7. It was fairly costly to have the sacraments/ceremonies of the church performed. For example in 1838 the following was the schedule of fees:

RECTOR'S FEES
(from The Jamaica Almanac, 1838, Call No. 4307.85, Rare Book Section, Boston Public Library)

Fees for:	£	S	D
Baptism in Church on Sunday	0	5	0
In another place or on any other day	1	0	0
For traveling to perform service		10	0
Marriages on Sunday by Banns	1	6	8
In any other place	4	0	0
By license	2	13	4
Funerals at Parochial	1	6	8

You can see why ex-slaves and poor whites married by banns, whereas rich people could afford licenses. Also baptism not at the church was expensive for it included not only a double fee, but also a fee for the rector to travel to the site.

Patricia Jackson has developed a website Jamaican Family Search at http://jamaicanfamilysearch.com/ . This site has many free pages but also has member pages for a modest fee. For example in 2006 it costs $8.00 US for a month and $70.00 US for a year to join. On the site she has a section on Jamaican Registers and Wills: Church of England and other [sources]:Extractions from Registers and Wills. On members pages there are many names which have been extracted from the Registers into this section. In June 2006 there were 246,400 names listed on the site and a great number of these are in this section on Jamaican Registers. There is a search function on the page at the bottom of the webpage so that you can quickly find the pages which contain the names of interest. You might be lucky to find your ancestor already extracted from the registers, but you will want to verify by seeking your own copy from the Register. Patricia has a reference to the source but it is not the FHL film number. See http://jamaicanfamilysearch.com/Samples/bibliogr.htm . However it is possible to compare this list with the one on her site of FHL films (see page 13 of this book) to find the correct film number.

Other Church of England Records

Although they do not contain vital records the following sources may be of interest. More detail may be found in *Sources of Jamaican History* by K. E. Ingram (see History References).

• Society for the Promoting of Christian Knowledge. Minutes, letters and papers with material relating to Jamaica. 1698 - S.P.C.K. London.

• United Society for the Propagation of the Gospel. Journals, letters and reports. 1703 - U.S.P.G. London.

• Church Missionary Society. Papers relating to Jamaica. 1820 - C.M.S. London. These missionaries were particularly involved with the education of former slaves and the collection includes letters and papers of individual missionaries.

A book about the Church of England in Jamaica is*: Roots and Blossoms* by Edmund Davis (Bridgetown, Barbados: Cedar Press, 1977, 124 pp). The early chapters cover the period before a bishop was appointed to the island in 1824. After that there are several chapters devoted to how the church coped with the lack of ministers and the early attempts to train upper class creoles to fulfill the clergy needed to meet parish needs. Quite a few chapters are devoted to the establishment of St Peter's Theological College and the many trials that were encountered. The author's main criticism is that the early curriculum was so dictated by the traditional classical background expected in English Public Schools (Greek and Latin) and not enough emphasis on the practical aspects and cultural forms of the people to whom they were going to administer. Few of the early applicants who were native Jamaicans therefore were matriculated into the College. He ends at the time the United Theological College was founded at the UWI, Mona in 1966.

Bishops' Transcripts (BT's)

In British research, if you can not find original parish records, you can fall back on Bishops' Transcripts. These were annual returns of baptisms, marriages and burials which the minister sent to his bishop, copies of which have been deposited in this century in record offices. They are very useful for verifying illegible parish records or in cases where the parish records might be torn or missing. Because some of the early vital records in Jamaica were missing, I wondered if the same rule had applied to Jamaican ministers. I wrote to Mr. Jeremy Gibson whose book on Bishops' Transcripts describes where these can be found in

England, explaining and surmising that prior to the establishment of the Diocese of Jamaica in 1824, the jurisdiction would be the Bishop of London. He confirmed the latter, but informed me that unfortunately no Bishops' Transcripts were evidently sent from Jamaica to England from 1655 to 1824. I have seen the suggestion that some might exist in Lambeth Palace; however, I have not followed up on this lead. As you will recognize, after the establishment of the Diocese of Jamaica, essentially all the existing parish records in Spanish Town are the equivalent of Bishops' Transcripts.

Non-Conformist Records

As you have probably guessed, there are fewer vital records available for all religious faiths other than Anglican in Jamaica. The following list gives the time frame for when the various groups were established in Jamaica, thus explaining, in part, why there are fewer resources.

Jews:	1500s-
Roman Catholics:	1494-1655, 1792-
Quakers:	1679-1749
Moravians:	1754
Baptists:	1782
Methodists:	1816
Presbyterians:	1824

(Jews also are treated in this book under the Emigration section.)
The Anglican church called non-conformists "dissenters" and in the nineteenth century required, particularly, marriages to be registered with the Diocesan Office. Perhaps this was because of Lord Hardwicke's Marriage Act of 1752, which required all dissenters other than Jews and Quakers to be married in a Church of England. However, in Jamaica by 1818 they did not have to be married in the Established church, but the Dissenter ministers had to send in returns to the Bishop of Jamaica (Anglican). Because of this requirement there are records in the Registrar General's Office (Island Record Office) at Spanish Town on Dissenter Marriages, and a small section on Dissenter Births. Most of these records are for Baptists, Methodists and Presbyterians. So far I have not seen reference to Dissenter Burials; however, there is a short series of deaths during the same period (1844-1854) as births (see below) which may cover some dissenters. The LDS church has filmed these registers (FHL Catalog: Jamaica/Church Records). There is no complete index for the entire Dissenter Marriage series, but volumes 16

through 20 covering the period 1870 to 1880 have a single index film reference. Also, at the front of most volumes there is an index, but unfortunately the volumes overlap in dates; therefore it is necessary to search several films to cover completely the time period of interest. Registers are not segregated by denomination, but were recorded as they came in to the Diocesan Office. However, the Dissenter Marriage registers have a significant amount of information including the name of the witnesses (potential family members) and the minister and where he was located in addition to names and ages of participants. The earliest dissenter marriages are for 1818 (sparse) but really begin in 1834, just after emancipation. They continue up to 1880 and Civil Registration.

The Dissenter Birth records which have been filmed cover a much shorter period (1844-1854, FHL Catalog: Jamaica/Church Records) than the Dissenter Marriage registers. In fact I am not sure that these records only include dissenters, because I have found a record in this section where the presiding minister was a Minister of the Church of England. Notice also that these are recorded as births not baptisms. There is a short index film which refers to these births (FHL Catalog: Jamaica/Civil Registration). There are also two films with Death Registers for the period 1844-54, which may contain dissenter deaths. (I have not examined them.) My supposition is that these records were the result of a short-lived attempt to start Civil Registration in Jamaica in 1844. (England had begun this in 1837.) However, the attempt was not successful, and the law was repealed in 1851. I think that explains two things: the fact that the records are births not christenings and deaths not burials, and that they contain mixed Anglican and non-conformist records. Also they were recorded on preprinted forms such as was required in England for Civil Registration.

The only other vital records which to my knowledge have been deposited publicly are some by the Wesleyan Methodist Church, by Jews in Kingston, and by the Moravian church. All others, if still held, are in the hands of the respective denominations.

Methodists

Among other Methodist church records which are found in the Jamaica Archives at Spanish Town (Ref. file 5/6, circa 65 items), the vital records have not been filmed and cover only a limited area and time period. They are:

Kingston Baptisms:	1824-1867, 1829-1902, 1838-1876
Port Royal Baptisms:	1838-1876
Spanish Town Marriages:	1829-1840

Patricia Jackson has developed a website Jamaican Family Search at http://jamaicanfamilysearch.com/. This site has many free pages but also has member pages for a modest fee. On one of her free pages http://jamaicanfamilysearch.com/Samples/Resjam.htm there is a list of Methodist records in the Jamaican Archives, Spanish Town. This includes many more Methodist records which have been deposited. So far they have not been extracted or microfilmed. They include in addition to Kingston, Port Royal and Spanish Town, Falmouth, St Ann's Bay, Stony Hill, Watsonville St Ann, Montego Bay Lucea and Brown's Town St Ann. These include baptisms and marriages but no burials. The site gives the dates. I hope someday these records will be available on line.

The Dissenter Records of the Anglican Diocese listed above have almost as many Methodist records as those of Baptists.

A modern history of Thomas Coke, 1747-1814, chronicles not only the life of Coke but also the early years of the Methodist church, especially in Kingston; the book is titled *Thomas Coke and the Early History of Coke Memorial Church, 1789-1839* by John W. Poxon (1989, 71 pp., published as a Bicentenary Publication by the Methodist District). This book unfortunately has no index, although the book mentions many parishioners by name. John Poxon was a Methodist minister and re-established York Castle School in Brown's Town, St. Ann in the 1950s.

Additional Methodist records which may be of interest, especially if your ancestor was a missionary, are:

• Methodist Missionary Society. Papers relating to Jamaica from the late eighteenth century to the first quarter of the twentieth century (more than 100 document boxes). Includes a biographical file of missionaries. More information on the persons to whom letters are addressed, missionary and non-missionary, are found in *Sources of Jamaican History* by K. E. Ingram (see History References).

• Methodist collections in England are housed in the John Rylands University Library, Manchester, and in London.

• Methodist Archives
C/O Archivist or Librarian, John Rylands University Library, Deans Gate, Manchester I13 9PL, England.
http://rylibweb.man.ac.uk/data1/dg/text/method.html

• Mrs. Joy Fox, Archivist for the Overseas Division, Methodist Church Overseas Division, 25 Marylebone Road, London NW1 5JR, England.

Jews

Vital records of Jews in Kingston, Jamaica have been filmed by the LDS Church (FHL Catalog: Jamaica/Jewish Records). This film includes a record of Jews from various sources and comes from St. Thomas, the Virgin Islands. It includes:

- Jamaican Birth Records, 1800s-1950
- Jamaican Circumcision Records, 1800s
- Jamaican Marriage Records, 1788-1920
- West Indian Grave Registration, 1809-ca.1850
- Jamaican Death Records, 1796-1824

You need to be able to read Hebrew to use this record, because the surnames are in Hebrew. The film is rather dark in some areas.

Patricia Jackson has obtained copies of many Jewish records in Jamaica. Her web pages which can be searched for a modest fee ($8 for a month, etc) are shown on free page http://jamaicanfamilysearch.com/Samples/jewish.htm. These include:

- Births in the Sephardic Congregation, Kingston, 1809-1902
- Marriages in the Sephardic Congregation, Kingston 1809-1901
- Deaths in the Sephardic Congregation, Kingston1809-1901
- Births in the Ashkenazi Congregation, Kingston 1789-1906
- Marriages in the Ashkenazi Congregation, Kingston 1788-1901
- Records of the Amalgamated and United Congregations, Kingston. From the records of the Amalgamated congregation 1883-1921 and the United Congregation of Isreaelites 1921-1963
  Births 1884-1930
  Marriages 1883-1945
  Deaths 1883-1963
- Tombstones in the Falmouth Jewish Cemetery
- Montego Bay Jewish records
- Synagogue leaders 1850
- Tombstones of some Jamaican Jews in New Orleans

An address in Jamaica which might yield some information as to where to search:

Jewish Community Synagogue, 92 Duke Street, Kingston, Jamaica, West Indies

See also Emigration.

Roman Catholics

From the time of Columbus until the conquest by Britain, the established religion of Jamaica was Roman Catholicism. The early records 1494-1655 are in depositories in Spain. After the British conquest, the church languished until 1792 when a chapel was established in Kingston to meet the spiritual needs of the Spanish, French, English and Irish Catholics in the island. Two books have been written relating the history of the church in Jamaica. The books are:

• *A History of the Catholic Church in Jamaica, BWI, 1494-1929* by Francis X. Delany, S.J. New York: Jesuit Mission Press, 1930, 292 pp. This book has a small number of names of Kingston parishioners, particularly illustrations of marriage records of Haitian refugees to Jamaica in the early 1800s. A copy of this book is held in the Latin American book section of the FHLibrary, Salt Lake City.

• *History of the Catholic Church in Jamaica* by Francis J. Osborne, S.J. Chicago, Illinois: Loyola University Press, 1988, 532 pp. (LC BX1455.2.O84, ISBN 0-8294-0544-5). (Has a map of Spanish Jamaica.) This book not only has a longer, more accurate account of the history of the church, but carries the history forward from 1930 to approximately 1978. It does not, however, mention the names of many parishioners, but mostly the missionaries and priests who built and expanded the church and Catholic schools in Jamaica.

Mentioned in this latter book as a documentary source are the Archives of the Catholic Archdiocese of Kingston, Jamaica. You might try writing to the Archbishop at the Archdiocese Office:

Archbishops Office, 21 Hopefield Avenue, Kingston 6, Jamaica, West Indies

or to the Bishop of Montego Bay to see if there are baptismal, marriage and burial records existing for your ancestor, but the church probably has few people to spare for much archival research, so do not expect a speedy response, if any. I am sure a donation is always welcome. The church has statistics on the number of baptisms, marriages and burials of Catholics in the island in this century, but I do not know the condition and extent of earlier nineteenth century records in the archives. Alternative exploration could be made with the appropriate Catholic rectory in the parish in which your ancestor lived. A 1985 phone book lists the following rectories: Balaclava, Black River, Brown's Town, Chapelton, Christiana, Falmouth, Highgate, Linstead, Lucea, Mandeville, Montego Bay, Morant Bay, Port Antonio, Porus, Reading, St. Ann's Bay, Sav-la-mar and Spanish Town, besides Kingston and St. Andrew rectories. The rector might refer you to the appropriate person in the archives or the Chancery Office (same address as the Archbishop) if the records do not exist at the rectory.

Patricia Jackson has done extensive extraction of the Roman Catholic Records for baptisms, marriages and burials of Jamaica. They can be seen on her site http://jamaicanfamilysearch.com. This is a site with a modest fee (in 2006, $8 US for a month) has a free page which describes the pertinent Roman Catholic records at: http://jamaicanfamilysearch.com/Samples/Catholic.htm . A print out of this page took 26 pages on a laser printer to show you how extensive the key to the transcription is. There are four sections of Roman Catholic records. The Registers in the first 3 sections are kept in the Roman Catholic Archives, Kingston, and are in the custody of the Revd. Gerard McLaughlin, Roman Catholic Chancery, 21 Hopefield Avenue, Kingston 6, Jamaica, West Indies. Patricia has a search function at the bottom of the page which will allow you to search for the surname. Most of the records are from Kingston and St Andrew, but later ones include records from other parishes. Some of the Kingston records are as early as 1798 and there are records available to 1901 but not all have been extracted as yet,(2006) It is an on going project. Records in Spanish and French have been translated into English. This is truly a great contibution to Jamaican genealogy.

There are a few records pertaining to Jamaica in the Westminster Cathedral Archives, Archdiocese of Westminster, London; however, most of these appear pertinent to the business of the church and do not seem to concern parishioner's records. Most of the correspondence pertains to the Eastern Caribbean and particularly Trinidad where the Vicar Apostolic resided. (See Ingram, *Sources of Jamaican History 1655-1838.*)

Quakers

A small group of Quakers were early settlers of Jamaica from England, particularly in St. Elizabeth, Westmoreland, Spanish Town and

Kingston, and are recorded from 1679 in Port Royal. Most of the Friends however left the island for Philadelphia, Pennsylvania (United States), by 1749 and only a few references to transferring lands previously owned by Quakers were recorded up to the 1790s. Some surnames include: Bird, Blake, Brown, Crosby, Davis, Dickenson, Elliet, Gale, Gunn, Hillyard, Moss, Noble, Norris, Pike, Pinnock, Richardson, Shittlewood, Taylby, Weamouth, Wellen, Willis and Willmott, among others. The Gale family was very prominent in St. Elizabeth. Minutes for the Meetings for Sufferings, Minutes of the Yearly Meeting, Letters Received and Sent and as well as some miscellaneous papers may be seen in the Society of Friends Library, London. More information on the documents available in the above library, including pages and volume numbers, may be found in *Sources of Jamaican History 1655-1838* by K. E. Ingram, described in the History Reference section of this book. Also detailed in Ingram is the Journal of the Life of Thomas Story a Quaker, who visited the West Indies including Jamaica (pp. 443-446 of source) in 1708. Story was apparently from Philadelphia or Burlington, PA. In this journal he describes meetings at the homes of Quakers in Kingston, Spanish Town and Port Royal, as well as the aftermath of the 1692 earthquake which was still evident. The Society of Friends, London, holds this journal. Another account is "Quakers and the Earthquake at Port Royal, 1692", *Jamaican Historical Review*, Vol. 8, pp. 19-31, 1971.

American researchers who cannot make the connection between Pennsylvania Quaker families and those in England might consider the possibility that their families made a home in Jamaica before removing to the United States. Any existing records would be in London, except for land patents and deeds of land sales that are in Jamaica. Burial grounds of Quakers in Jamaica are mentioned in the letters, but it is unlikely that any monumental inscriptions survive in Jamaica.

Moravians

The Moravians were the first non-conformist Protestant group to establish a community in Jamaica in 1754. This is described in an article in the *Jamaica Journal* entitled "The Moravians in Jamaica, from the Beginning to Emancipation, 1754 to 1838" by Fred Linyard (*Jamaica Journal*, Vol. 3, No. 1, 1969 March). Two Moravian plantation owners, Foster and Barham in Westmoreland, to convert the slaves to Christianity sought missionaries from England. The missionaries met much opposition from the surrounding proprietors and from the House of Assembly. Nonetheless, they did establish a church which exists today. For more information see K. E. Ingram, *Sources of Jamaican History*

1655-1838. There are also papers entitled "Moravian Church, Papers relating to the Jamaican Missions, 1754-1826", about 115 items, situated at Moravian Church House, London. Ingram reports that many of the letters are brittle, since the Moravian Church headquarters suffered damage in the London blitz during WWII. Additional books by J. H. Buchner, *The Moravians in Jamaica* (London 1854) and *The Breaking of the Dawn* (London 1904), are available as sources on Moravian Church history in Jamaica. I do not know if any of these sources contain vital records. A slim little book which is a lecture given by Richard S. Dunn in the James Ford Bell Lecture Series (No 32) is entitled *Moravian Missionaries at Work in a Jamaican Slave Community, 1754-1835* (Univeristy of Minnesota, 1994, 25pp) describes the Mission on Mesopotamia estate. Names of missionaries are given and a few slaves. Do not overlook the Dissenter Records of the Anglican Diocese listed above, since some of these records were Moravian.

On Patricia Jackson's free page: http://jamaicanfamilysearch.com/ Samples/moravia1.htm there is a list of Moravian Records from St Elizabeth transcribed by Robin Michelsen. These include baptism and receiving records for mostly ex-slaves from 1839-1845. For a small fee $8.00 US for a month you can access these records. They are interesting in their own right whether you are interested in St Elizabeth Moravian records, because they list prior slave names and baptism or reception name

The address of contact in Jamaica is: Moravian Church in Jamaica, Zorn Moravian Church Manse, Christiana, Manchester, Jamaica, West Indies

Baptists

The Baptists established their mission in Jamaica in 1814, although they had been in Jamaica from the late 1780s. (see *George Liele: Pioneer Missionary to Jamaica* by Clement Gayle. (Kingston, Jamaica: Jamaica Baptist Union. 1982/3. Bibliography, Appendix 47 pp. Written for the bi-centenial celebration of the Baptist establishment in Jamaica, this book describes the role that George Liele played in establishing the Baptists in Jamaica. He was a freed Slave from America and came to Jamaica in 1783 where he started to preach and baptize the slaves and ex-slaves in Kingston and surroundings. This book establishes that Liele and his followers were responsible for inviting the English

Baptist Mission to send representatives to the island who arrived in 1814. The appendix lists the covenant the early Baptists had. The text suggests why this early leader has been overlooked in the past.

The Baptist missionaries initial concern was bringing Christianity to the slaves and they were very active in the abolition of slavery. While I have not done a page count, the Dissenter Records of the Anglican Church listed above appear to have primarily Baptist records, which is fortunate since the Baptist church does not appear to have deposited its vital records publicly.

Inez Knibb Sibley (an author mentioned under Maps) was the descendent of a very active Baptist missionary, Rev Knibb, and besides a book on *Place Names of Jamaica* has written *The Baptists of Jamaica* (Jamaica: The Jamaica Baptist Union, 1965, 91 pp.). A copy of this book is held by the FHLibrary, Salt Lake City, in the Latin American Book Area. A well documented book about Knibb himself is *Knibb, 'the Notorious': Slaves Missionary 1803-1845* by Philip Wright. (London: Sidgwick & Jackson. 1973. ISBN 0-283-97873-3. 264 pp. illustrations, references and notes, index). The index lists many people especially ministers, and there are two illustrations of Knibb. A book about the Brown's Town, St. Ann, Baptist church and some of the early struggles, is *Goodness and Mercy: A Tale of A Hundred Years* by George E. Henderson, Pastor, 1876-1926, Brown's Town Baptist Church, Jamaica, BWI (1931, 173 pp., Kingston, Jamaica: The Gleaner Company Ltd. Lithographed Owen Sound, Ontario, Canada: Richardson, Bond & Wright Ltd., 1967). This book mentions many prominent Baptists in St. Ann and Trelawny; however it has no index. It also comments on some of the Baptists' confrontation with the Rev. George Bridges, Rector of St. Ann, of the Anglican Church.

A memoir written by a Baptist missionary is: *Bananaland: Pages from the Chronicles of an English Minister in Jamaica* by Ernest Price. London: The Carey Press 1930, 186 pp. photographs, no bibliography, no index. The missionary was Principal of Calabar College and Headmaster of Calabar High School

Some articles which relate to the Baptists in the *Jamaica Journal* are "The 19th Century Optimist of the Chapel: The Friendly Witness of James M. Phillippo, author of *Jamaica: Its Past and Present State*" as reviewed by James Carnegie (*Jamaica Journal*, Vol. 5, No. 1, pp. 11-15, 1971), and "Early Baptist Beginnings" by C. S. Reid (*Jamaica Journal*, Vol. 16, No. 2, pp. 2-8, 1983).

Records in London are held at the Baptist Missionary Society, London. Papers relating to Jamaica 1814-1900, about 200 items. These include letters, biographical material, copies of deeds and other papers. Some missionaries in these manuscripts include Coultart, Dendy, Knibb, Oughton, Phillippo, Tinson, Rowe as well as other laymen to whom letters were written. There is a list of 45 deeds throughout the island for 1816 to 1838 giving the Folio and Liber of the record in the Registrar General's Office. More information on this source may be seen in K. E. Ingram's *Sources of Jamaican History, 1655-1838* (see History References). Ingram also lists a number of printed sources which are based on manuscripts in this collection. The Baptist Missionary Society also has Committee minute books in six volumes which are indexed from 1819 to 1839 and includes matters such as appointments, retirements, acquisition of property for chapels, schools and other correspondence.

The address in Jamaica which might yield further information is:
Headquarters, The Baptist Union of Jamaica, 6 Hope Road, Kingston 10, Jamaica, West Indies

Presbyterians

The Presbyterians established their mission in Jamaica in 1824, 10 years prior to the abolition of slavery.

Some Presbyterian vital records are found in the Anglican Church Dissenter Records as described before. Otherwise I have not found references to this church and its vital records.

The British Society of Genealogists sells a book called *My Ancestors were English Presbyterians/Unitarians* by Alan Ruston (1993). In this book the author lists the following sources of documents for English Presbyterians:
Dr. William's Library, 14 Gordon Square, London, WC1H OAG, England

In addition to being a source of Methodist records, the following is a source of other non-conformist denominations:
John Rylands University Library of Manchester, Deansgate, Manchester, M3 3EH. England
http://rylibweb.man.ac.uk/data1/dg/text/method.html

Possible contact in Jamaica might be through:
The United Church of Jamaica and Grand Cayman, Office, 12 Carlton Crescent, Kingston 10, Jamaica, West Indies.

The above summarizes the main sources of information for vital records of denominations which were in Jamaica prior to Civil Registration which commenced in 1880. There are many other denominations currently in Jamaica. If you desire further church history concerning these twentieth century churches for your ancestor, I suggest you seek a contemporary Jamaica Telephone Book, Yellow Pages/Churches for addresses.

If you decide to write any of the denominations in Jamaica whose addresses are listed in this book, be as concise and brief as possible. Very few institutions in Jamaica are set up to respond to genealogists' queries, and most do not have the people available to do detailed searches if they do indeed have the records you seek. Copy machines may be unavailable or out of order so findings might be copied out longhand.

The primary concern is the current business of the denomination, not the past, so you will need to be very patient and understanding. Remember to send a self-addressed envelope. You might consider a donation to the work of the denomination, but consider it a gift not a fee for service.

 # Monumental Inscriptions

Another source of information on birth and death is an inscription on a tombstone or memorial tablet in a church or synagogue. Family historians in the U.S. and Britain lament the deterioration of MI's over time, but their temperate climates are relatively benign compared to the harsh climate of the tropics with respect to inscriptions. I have been into church cemeteries in the 1980s where there is nothing readable before 1890. If the memorial is inside a church or in a very well kept churchyard you might be lucky. Marble stones erode easily and the only stone which appears to withstand the sun, rain, moisture and growth well is granite. Unfortunately there is not a good source of granite in the island. My paternal grandparents' stones were pink granite, imported from Canada, and they are in very good condition, but the white island marble of my maternal grandmother has been covered with a black fungus which obscures the writing. All were buried in the 1940s.

Another source of deterioration is the practice particularly in public cemeteries of allowing people to tether their animals, chiefly goats, donkeys and cattle, in the cemetery. The animals may keep the bush in check, but the ropes of the animals wrap around the monuments and the standing stones are pulled down where they can be stepped on and broken up. In the public cemetery in St. Ann's Bay for instance, within a two year span, a stone that was standing had been pulled over and was so broken, it was no longer readable.

There were several animals in the grounds on each day I visited. Besides the risk of stepping in their excreta, the animals also enhance the population of ticks, which are the real hazard of rambling in cemeteries (or on plantation or estate burial grounds). Wear long pants tucked into socks and soak the latter with kerosene if you want to avoid an infestation of ticks. Not fun, I speak from experience.

Do not expect to find documentation on where the graves are placed in a cemetery. If you find an interested clergyman or gatekeeper who has been there for a while, you might get some help if you give a name, but don't be surprised if they leave you on your own to search.

At first many burials occurred in the churchyard surrounding a church. I have been trying to find out if there was any date setting up community parochial burial grounds, where the cemetery is divided into sections for different denominations, but there does not seem to be a consistent pattern, and it depends on the town and its resources.

Spanish Town, being the capital for many years, had several burial grounds which are referred to in vital records by numbers (i.e. No. 1 and No. 2). The May Pen cemetery is not in May Pen, Clarendon, but in Kingston. The Anglican churchyard in Port Royal was not very big (particularly after the 1692 earthquake). It appears that when they ran out of land Port Royal people buried their dead at sea; many references are made to burial at "the Palisades," but I know of no burial ground on that narrow spit of land. Alternatively they refer to "Green Bay" which was across the entrance to Kingston Harbour from Port Royal. So apparently the dead were transported by boat across the entrance. Prominent people from Port Royal may have been buried in Kingston.

When I lived in Kingston, actually Rest Pen, Half-Way-Tree, on the adjacent road West Kings House Road, there was a cholera cemetery. I never went into it, it was taboo (possibly because of fear of catching cholera) and terribly overgrown with bush, but I did hear that school boys of the time (1950s) thought it a big dare to get something from this cemetery in scavenger hunts. The walled cemetery at that time was more than 100 years old, since the cholera epidemic (worldwide) in which over 32,000 Jamaicans died was in 1849-50. I do not know if there were ever any monumental inscriptions, but the site has been demolished and is now a roundabout on a main arterial from upper St. Andrew into Kingston. There must have been others of this type over the island, which have completely disappeared.

Often there was a burial ground on an estate, since frequently it was too far away from a church, and bodies had to be put into the ground rapidly because there was no way to preserve them in the tropics. Such burial grounds may still exist, even if the estate has been broken up into small plots for settlement. However they are probably badly overgrown, and you may need a machete to chop your way through the tropical bush. Many of the MI's will have deteriorated in this surrounding, and I suspect that a large number of graves never had inscriptions. In one such burial ground near Brown's Town, St. Ann, there were two perfectly preserved tombs of brick standing about three feet high, but there was no evidence there had ever been a tablet of any kind. It was not possible to tell when the tombs had been erected. In the same burial ground one grave had beside it a lovely old large terra cotta pot, of the type used to plant lilies, which was still in perfect condition in the late 1980s although it was near a grave stone which was erected in 1878. Possibly the overgrowth and fear of "duppies" (ghosts) contributed to its still being there, since everything of that type is usually recycled in Jamaica.

Slaves may have been buried in the family burial ground or in land set aside especially for that purpose. But it is unlikely that any monuments were erected for slaves, at least any that were survivable.

There are three compilers who have attempted to document the Protestant memorials and monumental inscriptions of Jamaica. The last mentioned is the most complete and claims to have verified the citations of the other two. The three are Archer, Roby and Wright:

• *A Collection of all the Monumental inscriptions prior to 1750 in Barbadoes, also similar inscriptions in Jamaica* by J. H. L. Archer (1857-8. British Library Add. MS 23608 1 vol. 9-34ff.). James Henry Lawrence Archer was a captain in the 60th Rifles and was particularly interested in those inscriptions which pertained to his ancestors in Jamaica. Another book by him is *Monumental inscriptions of the British West Indies from the earliest date* by Lawrence-Archer, J. H. 1823-1889 *with genealogical and historical annotations, from original, local, and other sources, illustrative of the histories and genealogies of the seventeenth century, the calendars of state papers, peerages and baronetages; with engravings of the arms of the principal families.* Chiefly collected on the spot by Captain J.H. Lawrence-Archer. (London, Chatto and Windus), 1875. Patricia Jackson on her site has transcribed this book. http://jamaicanfamilysearch.com/. Of the 450 pp, Jamaica occupies 342 pp. An index to the Book is free at: http://jamaicanfamilysearch.com/Samples/Barcher2.htm. The full text is available to members for a modest fee (e.g. $8.00 per month in 2006). A general search function into which you can input your surname of interest is available on the site.

• Roby was the Collector of Customs and Postmaster of Montego Bay and as a hobby pursued genealogy and local history. He published *Monuments of the Cathedral Church and Parish of St. Catherine: being Pt 1 of Church Notes and Monumental Inscription of Jamaica in the year 1824* privately in Montego Bay, 1831. It is obvious from correspondence that he had with the historian C. E. Long and his friend Dr. James Miller that he collected further information, but this apparently was never published and his notes have not been found. A copy of this work is found in the RCS library.

• The most complete source is *Monumental Inscriptions of Jamaica* compiled by Philip Wright (London: Society of Genealogists, 1966, 361 pp.). This book is available on microfiche (7 fiche) from the SoG, London, for purchase, as well it may be viewed as the printed work in the library. The FHLibrary of Salt Lake City also has a printed copy in the Latin American Book area, and it has been microfilmed so is available through Family History Centers (FHL Catalog: Jamaica/Monumental Inscriptions). The inscriptions are compiled up to 1878, so they almost cover the period up to Civil Registration. While a great number of estate burial grounds and churches and church yards are covered, the latter are mainly Anglican, though some Non-Conformist churchyards are covered. No public burial grounds are included and no Jewish burial grounds (see below) are found in the list. The arrangement is by parish and an all-name index is found at the end of the book. Wright indicates where he did not personally verify the data obtained from Roby or Archer, in some cases because the inscription no longer existed in the 1960s.

Andrade, in his book on Jamaican Jews, *A Record of the Jews in Jamaica from the English Conquest to the present time* by Jacob A.P.M. Andrade (ed. by Basil Parke, Kingston, Jamaica: Jamaica Times, 1941, 282 pp., 2 maps), lists 23 burial places of Jews in Jamaica (pp. 100-101). In his appendices he lists epitaphs and memorials from many of these cemeteries (pp. 201-237). One was at Hunt's Bay, which is on the Kingston Harbour waterfront and in the 1980s a site of major development for container shipping. A *Daily Gleaner* article in the 1930s describes this as one of the oldest Jewish cemeteries in the island. The American Jewish Historical Society has an article on this cemetery: Silverman H.P., "The Hunt's Bay Jewish Cemetery, Kingston Jamaica BWI" (*American Jewish Historical Society*, Vol. 37: pp. 327-344, 1947). A copy of this article is found in the Commonwealth Library at Cambridge University, England. The inscriptions were in three languages: the native language (usually Portuguese), Hebrew and English. This cemetery still exists.

The Orange Street Jewish Cemetery in Kingston was in use from 1820 to 1979. There were also two Jewish burial grounds in Spanish

Town to which I have seen reference; one was known as the Mouk or
Monk St. Cemetery. Another cemetery is one situated at Gaza, Watson
Hill in Manchester (referenced in 1878 Jamaica Directory), and two in
Montego Bay; one of the latter I understand is still preserved and open to
the public. Falmouth in Trelawny also had Jewish burial grounds, since
there were quite a few Jewish families who settled there. Patricia
Jackson on her site http://jamaicanfamilysearch.com has transcribed the
tombstones of the Falmouth Jewish Cemetery and they are available on
her site for a modest fee. Photographs of the cemetery are also available.
G. R. Coulthard has published an article on "The Inscriptions on Jewish
Gravestones in Jamaica" in *Jamaica Journal* (Vol. 2, No. 1, pp. 8-9,
1968 March). This also pertains to the Hunt's Bay cemetery so applies to
1680 onwards. Another fuller article from the same journal is:
"Tombstones in the Jewish Cemetery and What They Tell" by Betty
Bailey with photographs by Ernest deSouza (*Jamaica Journal*, Vol. 20,
No. 2, pp. 17-22, 1987). This excellent illustrated article describes the
Orange Street, Kingston cemetery, which was in use up to 1979.

The most comprehensive book on Jewish monumental inscriptions
was published in 1997: *The Jews of Jamaica: Tombstone Inscriptions
1663-1880* by R. D. Barnett and P. Wright (Jerusalem: Ben Zvi Institute,
1997, 202 pp., ISBN 965-235-068-0). The material for this book was
collected by Philip Wright in the 1960s by photograph and was
retranslated (Hebrew inscriptions) and checked from the gathered
material for this edition. The inscriptions are from Hunt's Bay, Kingston,
Spanish Town, Annotto Bay, St. Ann's Bay, Falmouth, Montego Bay,
Lucea, Savanna-la-Mar, Lacovia and Rowe's Corner (Manchester), and
amount to some 1,456 inscriptions. As expected Kingston contributes the
largest number to the total, since this is where most Jews lived and died.
Note that this collection is comprised of inscriptions up to 1880.
Andrade lists some that extend beyond that date in Kingston. The older
inscriptions are given in Hebrew and/or Portuguese or Spanish, with
headings in English that give the pertinent burial information. There are
comprehensive indexes of names and dates. A few photographs are
included with an aerial view of Hunt's Bay cemetery in the introduction.

Some pre-1855 inscriptions in Kirkcudbrightshire Scotland which
pertain to Jamaican residents are to be seen on Patricia Jackson's site
http://jamaicanfamilysearch.com/. It is on a members page so requires a
small fee for access.

Probate Records

Wills and documents pertaining to probating a will can be very helpful in determining the relationships between family members with the same surname whose data you find in vital records. Most often the testator (maker of the will) used the terms "my daughters," "my sons-in-law," "my cousin" etc. with their names. Inventories of the personal estate (goods and chattels) can give a wonderful insight into how your ancestor lived, and the will itself may show what items among the ancestor's possessions he or she thought the most valuable things. For example in the 1600s to early 1700s certain childbed linens were often listed in inventories and left to daughters in wills.

In Jamaica wills were made from the earliest time after the English conquest in 1655. These early wills were probated in the Prerogative Court of Canterbury (PCC) in England, which ecclesiastical court had jurisdiction over wills where the estate (real or personal) was overseas as well as in England. Very soon after the establishment of a government in Jamaica, wills were deposited with the Island Secretary in the capital Spanish Town, and the first will book into which such a proven will was copied was in 1663. So there are wills of Jamaican families both in England and in Jamaica from the earliest times.

In 1858 the General Probate Registry was established at Somerset House in London for all English will probates, and wills were no longer proved in the PCC. By that time however wills from Jamaica were mainly probated in the Supreme Court of Jamaica, Spanish Town, and most of the wills in the middle to late nineteenth century were proved and recorded there unless the Jamaican also held land in England or died in England. For example, I have found a PCC will in 1854 of a man who was born and lived most of his life in Jamaica, but he died in England and had lease of a property in England as well as owned an estate in Jamaica.

It is worthwhile looking for a **will** even if your ancestor was of modest means and did not own land. His personal estate might have consisted of furniture and clothing and a horse. Even if he died intestate (without a will), he might have an **administration** (admon) or authority to administer the property of a deceased person, in which case an **inventory** of his property would have been made. Both administrations and inventories were also recorded for people who had wills. Another probate document was a **letter testamentary** which authorized the executors of a will to act. All these types of documents are helpful to different degrees to family historians, the letter testamentary being minimal for it only identifies the executors and the approximate date of death. The PCC has admons but apparently not many inventories were kept. I have only seen reference to letters testamentary in Jamaica.

Slaves did not make wills, but free people of colour probably did, so it would be fruitless to look for wills of African ancestors prior to 1834 (emancipation) for slaves or prior to about 1760s for free people of colour. However, wills and inventories of whites who owned slaves should be of great interest because (a) often the white master in his will freed his personal slave or servant, his mistress and her children by him, or a specially skilled slave (e.g. a cooper) to whom he had promised his freedom, and (b) inventories, at least early ones, often listed by name the slaves owned by the white proprietor at his death.

In the indexes I have seen there are not as many women as men who made wills, because until the 1880s married women's property belonged to their husbands. There are some wills of women however both in the PCC and in the Jamaican records, mostly those of widows with daughters. I have not come across any of older single women, probably because most property descended to a male heir, cousins, etc., and it was rare not to be able to find such an heir. Also I suspect very few women remained unmarried in the scarce market for suitable white women in Jamaica. Still it is worthwhile checking for a woman's will, especially if she was a widow and could have owned property. If a widow married again, the property she inherited could go to her second husband to dispose of, unless her second husband also died before she did, or if she had a son by her first husband, or if the first husband had stipulated otherwise in *his* will.

While all PCC wills (England and Jamaica) have been microfilmed and are available through the LDS Library in Salt Lake City, and are available on-line from the National Archives Kew London, none of the early Jamaican probate documents at Spanish Town have been filmed to my knowledge (exception: the Supreme Court wills — see later). The only way to search for them is in Spanish Town, by finding a person to do it for you. There are some indexes to wills which are available to help delineate the search.

Prerogative Court of Canterbury (PCC)

Index

An index to wills probated in the PCC of Englishmen owning property in Jamaica, or of Jamaican property owners who also owned property in England, or by people in Jamaica who considered it a sign of status, was compiled by Oliver in *Caribbeana*. (See History References, also on LDS film.) This list starts in 1655 and goes up to 1816, so you can see that it does not quite cover the full period before the General Probate Registry was established in England in 1858. Thus if the period you want is between 1816 and 1858, you'll need to consult a British genealogical aid to find indexes and wills of the PCC. The lists are scattered throughout *Caribbeana*, since they were compiled over the period 1909-1916 and are not in a single issue, so you will need to search the whole film for the complete list up to 1816. I should remark that I found a will in the PCC which was *not* included in the *Caribbeana* list. This was a will for a woman who died in London in 1727 who had lived in Jamaica and had property in Jamaica. I first found reference to the will in manuscripts in the British Library. I do not know if Oliver overlooked it because it was the will of a woman or if it was just an oversight. Thus a warning is in order if you do not find your ancestor's will in the *Caribbeana* index to the PCC: it may still exist and you may need to search the English indexes to the PCC. You may also know there is no general index in England for PCC wills between 1700-1750, so one needs to search individual volume indexes.

The index in *Caribbeana* gives the year, the volume by name, and the folio (actually "quire") e.g. 1750, (Bushby, 36). A folio/quire held about 8-16 wills and there were usually no page numbers within a folio. The PCC is distinguished by the fact that the volumes or libers were known and indexed by the name of the most important testator who appeared in that volume. For a more detailed discussion of PCC wills, indexes, etc., see Miriam Scott, "Prerogative Court of Canterbury: Wills and Other Probate Records" (Public Record Office Readers' Guide No. 15, 1997), or on-line for all English wills you can find information at: http://www.catalogue.nationalarchives.gov.uk/RdLeaflet.asp?sLeafletID =168

On-Line PCC Wills and Index

The National Archives at Kew, London (formerly the PRO, Public Record Office) has on-line search for PCC Wills for all years.1383-1858. It is located at: http://www.documentsonline.nationalarchives.gov.uk/. A search function allows you to enter the name, date, occupation and place. Try all the known cognates/variations of the person in the name blank before giving up on finding the will. Try leaving out Jamaica if you get no results, because the person could have died in England without property in Jamaica or the will may not have had the place name Jamaica in the introduction to the will. Once you find the will you can down load it for a modest cost (currently in 2005 it costs £3.50 to down load most wills).

At the World Gen Web Jamaica site http://www.rootsweb.com/ ~jamwgw/early.htm. I have listed an Index to Early Wills of Jamaica. These include PCC wills, 1655-1816 taken from the Caribbeana index lists discussed above. You can then check them with the National Archives Documents on line and down load the actual wills to your desktop. Note this index only goes to 1816, but does concentrate on Jamaica. The full index from the National Archives on-line goes from the 1383 up to 1858.

Wills

Once you find the will in the index you can down load it for a modest cost (currently in 2005 it costs £3.50 to down load most wills) from Documents on line at the National Archives Kew, London at. http://www.documentsonline.nationalarchives.gov.uk/. See above in indexes.

Alternately with the information on the year, volume and folio, you can search the FHL Catalog (England\Probate\PCC) for the correct film number and you can order a photocopy of the will from the FHLibrary in Salt Lake City on the appropriate form. You need to find the film number yourself in order to fill out the form correctly, and it is wise to make a note on the form that "pages within a folio/quire are not given in the PCC."

The record you will receive is a copy of the will transcribed into the record book, not the original will, so keep this in mind. When I have had the opportunity to compare the copy record to the original will in the PCC, the major points are very accurate; some small errors or changing in name may occur, e.g. in one the name was Joan in the other Joannah.

Scribes did not put the emphasis on correct spelling that we do today and in the same will you can find several spellings of the same place name. The Probate paragraph assigning responsibility to the executors is in Latin in the PCC.

Admons

Admons or Administrations in the PCC of Jamaican people who died intestate are not indexed in *Caribbeana* as wills are. Therefore you will need to look at the British PCC records in the FHL Catalog for indexes to admons and there is no way of knowing if the person was from Jamaica. When you find the possible name you can then order the appropriate film with the admon from the FHLibrary.

Admons in the PCC are usually written entirely in Latin, as is the Probate paragraph of wills, but you can usually discern the Latinized version of the name for which you are seeking.

Registrar General's Office/Archives Jamaica

Supreme Court Wills

Very few of the probate records existing in the Registrar General's Office and National Archives in Jamaica have been filmed. However, in August 1997, the FHL Catalog listed the first series of films that are available, under Jamaica/Probate. These six films are Supreme Court wills from 1725 to 1930, with some gaps. The first film in the series 1725-1882 actually goes from 1775 to 1882 and includes very few wills before 1840. The wills filmed are the actual wills and not the enrolled series that constitutes the bulk of the wills described later.

Patricia Jackson on her site has indexes of the wills of the Supreme Court. http://jamaicanfamilysearch.com/Members/Registers.htm. She has these indexes on a members page, so for a modest fee you can access them. (In 2006, $8.00 for a month) Each will appears alphabetically by last name and chronologically within a group of years of probate. There are handwritten addenda in the margins of many of these wills which record when real estate was entered in the title of deeds. Some of the items were added five to 20 years after the will was probated. This might explain the series of *actual* wills. The wills also have marked on them the date of enrollment in the records. One thing this suggests is that if a person did not leave real estate but only personal property, the will might exist in enrolled form but not as the actual will. Some of the wills are typed and obviously prepared in a lawyer's office; some of them are in the original handwriting of the testator. The quality of the wills varies; some bleed through of ink makes some wills difficult to read. The FHL Catalog lists these wills as 1725-1930.

Wills in Jamaica

Indexes

There are three sources for looking up locations of wills recorded or enrolled in Jamaica:

1. The National Archives or Registrar General's Office holds an index to wills. You need to know the year of death or approximate time and the parish to use it efficiently. The index gives the liber (volume) and folio (pages) of the will record; e.g. a will of 1777 was found in Liber 44, Folio 207. Because some of the early will books deteriorated some of them have been recopied and the original folio in the index may no longer be valid unless it says old folio, new folio.

2. *Caribbeana* (See History References) has a printed index to wills "which are on record in the Office of the Island Secretary, Jamaica from 1663-1750." These indexes were compiled by Vere Oliver from the third source below. They occur throughout *Caribbeana*; therefore it is necessary, as with the PCC will index mentioned before, to search the six volumes on film of *Caribbeana* for these lists. The first list, 1663-1700, is ordered by liber with several years in each liber. The names are not alphabetical. The second list is alphabetically ordered within each year for the period 1731-1750. The folios are not given for these indexes. I have not found the list which covers the period 1700-1730 in *Caribbeana*, but I have only had access to the film.

3. A third source is available in the British Library (Ad MS 21,931): handwritten lists compiled by the Jamaican historian C. E. Long. These lists cover the period 1661-1750 and are described as follows: List 1, 1661-1700 by liber without folio non-alphabetical; List 2, 1700-1730, alphabetically by year and liber, with folio numbers; List 3, 1731-1750 alphabetically by year with liber and without folio.

The third source has been used to compile the Early Wills of Jamaica included on the World Gen Web Jamaica site at:

http://www.rootsweb.com/ ~ jamwgw/early.htm. Unfortunately it is very difficult to get hold of copies of these wills. You will have to try to get a records researcher in Jamaica. David Bromfield on his web page http://www.bromfield.us/ offers a service with Wayne Burnside to search wills and other probate records. You will find a description of the records that Wayne searches and the fees on David Bromfield's site. It is a fairly expensive search option but less than a trip to Jamaica! It is possible to negotiate the fees with Wayne via his e-mail address.

Recorded Wills and Original Wills

The wills in the volumes of the Island Record Office were all written in English from the earliest times, 1661. It must be remembered that these were copied into the record books and spelling of the early wills may be inconsistent. Some of the early will books have been recopied because of deterioration, and thus there were two opportunities for errors to creep in. According to Ingram, *Sources of Jamaican History*, in 1926 there were 137 volumes of wills enrolled in the Registrar General's Office. In addition he notes that there are 93 boxes of original wills dating from 1724-1899, and two boxes of will bonds 1829-1847. The latter wills are most probably the Supreme Court wills referred to above, with additions made to 1930.

Inventories

Inventories were made usually by two upstanding men of the community after the death of a man, often being shown the personal property (not real property, i.e. real estate) by the man's widow. The estimated value in pounds, shillings and pence is given of nearly each item, so in addition to showing the lifestyle of the owner, it is interesting to see what various items were worth at the time. Early inventories were particularly revealing because they listed all the slaves by name, often divided into categories, e.g. able-bodied men, feeble old women, young boys, etc., and the values by category were given. On plantations often all the tools used in various parts of manufacturing sugar and rum were named and valued. In one inventory of 1717 of St. Elizabeth, I came across this listing in the Overseer's House: "bed linen of the white servants." I found this of interest not only because today we would not list bed linens as an important asset, but also because it showed that there were still white servants (probably indentured) in 1717 and that they obviously slept at the Overseer's House not the main house.

Men of the time were expected to join militias if the island was threatened, so often the inventory listed their guns and ammunition.

Books were not very plentiful in inventories, and besides a special Bible which might be named, were usually compiled as "a box of books."

Indexes

There are index volumes to the deceased for whom inventories are available in the Registrar General's Office, Spanish Town. Reference 1B/11.

Recorded Inventories

There are more than 160 volumes of enrolled inventories in the Registrar General's Office in Spanish Town, Ref 1B/11. They date from 1674 to the 1880s at least. Ingram notes that there were three volumes missing, Volume 4 (1695-1698), Volume 7, and Volume 8 (1706-1709). In addition there are some original inventories of 1775-1881 in 20 boxes. I do not know if these original inventories have been indexed.

Administrations (Admons) and Accounts

Administration of property under a will was granted to the executors by the governor or his representative. These records can be found in the Registrar General's Office, Ref 1B/11. The accounts arising from the administration are also found in the RGO, although they are of a shorter series than those of administrations, also Ref 1B/11. The accounts can be of interest in showing the debts the deceased had at his time of death, which had to be paid by the executors.

Indexes

There are three index volumes to Letters of Administration and two index volumes to Accounts. This covers up to 1838, so the series of indexes are likely to be more extended than indicated.

Letters of Administration and Accounts Current of Trustees or Administrators, Jamaica

Letters of Administration from 1710 to 1842 exist in 41 volumes. Ingram gives a list of the years which each of these volumes covers. The series probably continues past 1842.

Also in the above source Accounts Current of Trustees or Administrators, Jamaica, are listed as occupying 40 volumes from 1809 to 1838. In addition there are two boxes of Accounts Current, from 1780 to 1897. Therefore it is likely that the enrolled series extends past the date given above.

Testamentary

Letters Testamentary for Jamaica are also found in the RGO, Ref 1B/11. These letters are of the enrollment of the authorization of the executors to act. There are 51 volumes, including two index volumes covering the period 1716-1838. Also Ingram notes that Volume 5, 1732-1739, includes Letters of Guardianship. It is likely that this series extends to a later date than is indicated here.

Family Papers

As a source of wills you should not overlook collections of family papers which exist in various record depositories, mainly in the United Kingdom. K. E. Ingram in *Sources of Jamaican History* (in sections 10 and 11, items 425 to 749) lists alphabetically the manuscript sources of family papers which have been deposited and some of their contents which often include wills and accounts of estates as well as letters written to and by family members. The wills and other probate documents found in these collections may be the original wills or copies made by lawyers and secretaries, especially where there were legal disputes.

Three Maps

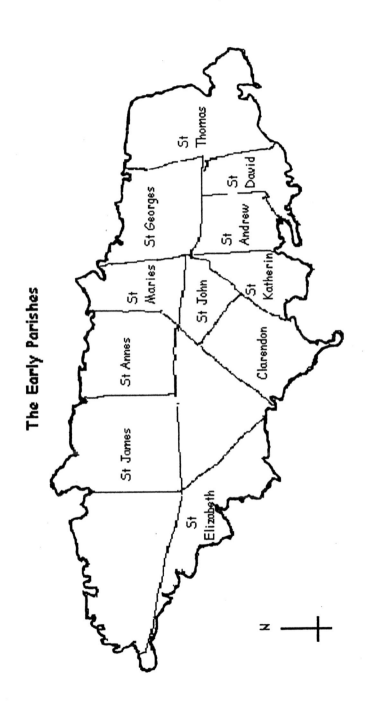

The Early Parishes

St Thomas

St David

St Georges

St Andrew

St Maries

St John

St Katherin

St Annes

Clarendon

St James

St Elizabeth

N

The Parishes in 1844

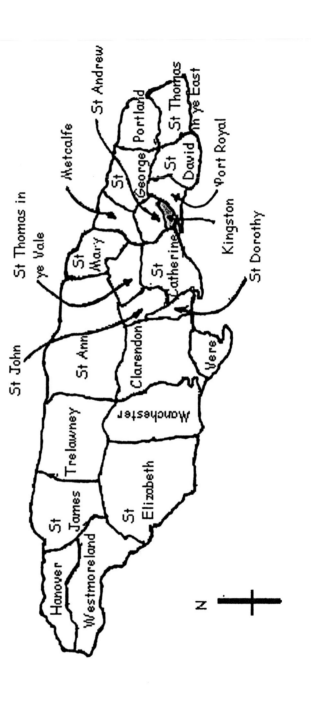

St Andrew

St Thomas

Portland

George

St Thomas in ye East

St

David

Port Royal

Metcalfe

St

Kingston

St Thomas in ye Vale

St Mary

St Catherine

St Dorothy

St John

St Ann

Clarendon

Vere

Trelawney

Manchester

St James

St Elizabeth

Hanover

Westmoreland

N

The Present Parishes

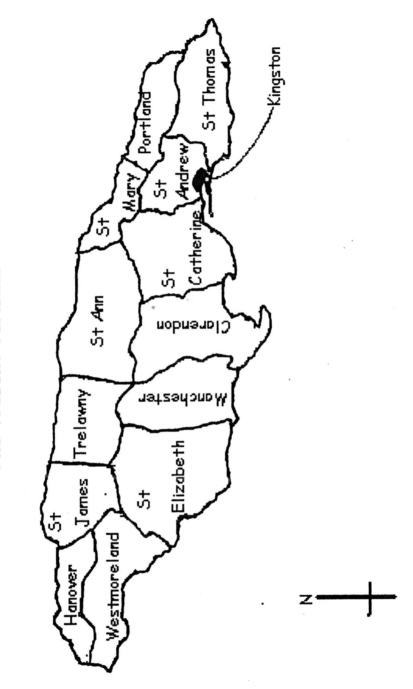

Maps
and
Prints

Maps are essential for genealogists and Jamaica has many of them. There are original maps on the market at steep prices from dealers in maps, but the family historian would be happy with map reproductions. So far I have not found a good source for reproduced maps of Jamaica, so most of my collection has been photocopied.

Jamaica is divided into three counties from west to east, namely Cornwall, Middlesex and Surrey. However very few records were collected on the basis of the county, so most of your work will be on the parish or the whole island. The number of parishes has changed over the years. The current parishes are: Hanover, St. James, Trelawny, St. Ann, St. Mary, Portland, St. Thomas, Kingston, St. Andrew, St. Catherine, Clarendon, Manchester, St. Elizabeth and Westmoreland. Additional parishes were: Vere, St. John, St Dorothy, St. Thomas in the Vale, St. David, Metcalfe, St. George. The maps on previous pages show the current and all former parishes. In the section on church/vital records, there is information on when the parishes were formed, dissolved or reabsorbed into various parishes.

Local administration of a parish was governed by a Vestry, which was an elected board of 12 men, comprised of the Custos Rotolorum (Chief Magistrate) as chair, the Rector and two churchwardens and various magistrates.

Sources of Maps

• *The Printed Maps of Jamaica up to 1825* by Kit S. Kapp (London: Map Collectors Circle, 1968, 36 pp.). A copy of this book is in the FHLibrary in Salt Lake City (FHL Catalog: Jamaica/Maps/Bibliography, no microfilm), and in the NLJ. The Commonwealth Library at Cambridge

University, England, also has a copy. The text details where the maps may be found in collections.

• *Jamaica in Maps* by C. G. Clarke (London: London University Press, 1974, 104 pp.). I have not seen this book, but it looks more extensive than the above and is available in the RCS library in Cambridge, England.

• *Maps and Plans in the Public Record Office: 2. America and West Indies* edited by P. A. Penfold (London: H.M. Stationery Office, 1974, 835 pp.). (Out of print.) Contains lists of about 142 manuscript and printed maps of Jamaica including counties, town and estates — eighteenth and nineteenth centuries.

Major Maps

The first map which is useful for genealogy because it shows plantations with names of owners or occupiers is that of **Craskell & Simpson, 1763**. Thomas Craskell was Island Engineer and the builder of King's House, and James Simpson was a Surveyor. These maps show the location of the Army Barracks in the interior of the island where soldiers were stationed against the Maroons between the Maroon Wars. It also shows how sparsely inhabited the interior of the island was at that time.

Robertson's Maps of Jamaica printed in 1804 mentioned in Lady Nugent's Journal show the growth in the settlement of the island between 1763 and 1800. James Robertson was a Scotsman who was listed as a surveyor in commission in Jamaica between 1793 and 1810. His maps were based on surveys and have such detail that sugarworks are designated by little icons as wind or cattle powered. Names of proprietors as well as plantation names are used. Robertson made four maps altogether: one of each of the counties of Cornwall, Middlesex and Surrey, and one of the entire island. The maps were printed in London.

In 1824 the Diocese of Jamaica of the Anglican Church was formed with a Bishop of Jamaica appointed. A map of the island showing the main parish churches in the capitals of the parishes and the associated chapels was made. This is important in understanding the vital records of the parishes. The rector was located at the parish church, and the island curates or stipendiary curates traveled to the chapels to perform christenings, marriages and burials. The curates then sent, in a group, copies of the records to the rector, who entered them in the parish records. Thus the vital record taken together with this map can identify the district in a parish where your subject lived, if it was not in a town.

Chapels in this map were congregations of the Established Church, the Church of England, and not, as some have later assumed, dissenter chapels. Later many became churches with a rector or vicar of their own. For example, St. Mark's Chapel in Brown's Town, St. Ann, later became St. Mark's Church. A copy of this map, which I call the Diocese Map of 1824 but which is simply called *Jamaica*, is located in the FHLibrary at Salt Lake City.

The most useful map I own is a 1927 map which belonged to my paternal grandfather that my father gave me. My father used it extensively in traveling about the island as an Agriculture Officer. The map, entitled *MAP of JAMAICA: prepared from the Best Authorities 1927*, was prepared in the Public Works Department by Colin Liddell, Acting Government Surveyor, 26th January 1888, Revised July 1905 by Liddell and Corrected to 1926 by the Public Works Department. The 3rd edition of the map has great detail on property, estate, settlement and village locations as well as showing the roads, Jamaica Railway, post offices, police stations, churches and chapels. I have not seen an earlier edition so I do not know how extensive the revisions were from 1888.

A modern map such as those sold by gasoline (petrol) stations (Esso, Texaco) is useful to determine present chief towns and locations if you are going to visit the sites of your ancestors, but most do not have the detail of the 1927 map listed above.

A more detailed set of contoured maps was prepared by aerial survey in 1968, and preliminary editions of this survey were published by the government of Jamaica in 1973, called *Jamaica 200, Preliminary Edition*. These very large maps were printed by the Survey Department of Jamaica, and I believe they are available in Spanish Town, Jamaica. They are rather cumbersome to use for genealogical purposes, since the sheets are very large, but they are able to pinpoint fine detail. An account of this Cadastral Survey is given in "The Cadastral Survey" by Phillip Rose (*Jamaica Journal*, Vol. 8, No. 1, pp. 37-41, 1974).

The bauxite companies of Jamaica in the 1950s and '60s when they were purchasing land for mining or land resettlement did detailed evaluations with maps of who had title to the land in which they were interested. These collections would be invaluable to the family historian even though they only cover those parts of the island in which bauxite was mined. Many of the old plantations and pens were divided by that time into small settlements, the deeds of which may be difficult to trace without such valuable maps. It is to be hoped that the companies will deposit the maps in the Archives rather than dispose of them when they are no longer of use.

A very important map to those with African ancestry is the map in the *History of Jamaica* p. 74, by Clinton Black (see History References), which shows the locations in **West Africa from which Jamaican slaves** were seized. The districts of different tribes, e.g. Ebo (Ibo), Coromantee, Mandingo, as well as the ports from which they were shipped, are shown. Modern maps would then be consulted to determine the current name of the country, e.g. Nigeria, Ghana, Liberia, Gambia, Congo.

Clinton Black's *History*, p. 27, also has a map showing the extent of occupation of the island of Jamaica by the **Spanish** from 1494-1655.

The National Library of Jamaica has a very large collection, estimated at about 20,000, of estate plans and plantation maps. Many of them simply show the boundaries of lands deeded or patented with the names of owners and adjacent proprietors. These can be very useful since relatives often owned adjoining properties. Some, however (about 1,000), are estate maps made by surveyors with cartographic illustrations and detail including the names of fields, etc. In addition the buildings and structures such as aqueducts for the sugar works may be shown. About 142 of the latter have been assembled in *Jamaica Surveyed: Plantation maps and plans of the eighteenth and nineteenth centuries* by B. W. Higman (Kingston, Jamaica: Institute of Jamaica Publications Limited, 1988, 307 pp.). More than just maps, illustrations include prints of houses and modern photographs of the existing structures or sites. The examples covered include: sugar estates, coffee, pimento and cotton plantations and pens. Some biographical information on the owners as well as the chief surveyors are given, and the relationships between different partners of surveyors. At one plantation, the plots assigned to slaves, their names and mothers' names are given, illustrating the use which can be made of slave returns and plantation records in determining family structure. Illustrations of garden plots assigned to apprentices are also used.

On-line Maps
On the WorldGenWeb page I have a contemporary map and two large maps of 1886 at:http://www.rootsweb.com/~jamwgw/jammaps.htm. Also on the page is a link which shows the historical development of the parishes http://prestwidge.com/river/jamaicanparishes.html with several links to actual early maps Patricia Jackson also has maps on her site.

Place Names of Jamaica, Buildings and Photographs

The origin of the place names shown in maps of Jamaica is covered in a lovely little book *Dictionary of Place-Names in Jamaica* by Inez Knibb Sibley (Kingston, Jamaica: Institute of Jamaica, 1978, 193 pp.). Inez Sibley was the great-granddaughter of William Knibb, a Baptist missionary who was an advocate of the slaves. This work is not just a list of place names but often contains snippets of genealogy which may be helpful. For example, the lengthy description of May Pen opens

> MAY PEN, capital of Clarendon, was one part of a property owned by the Rev. William May, who was born in Ash, Kent, England in August, 1695, and educated at St. John's College, Cambridge. When he came to Jamaica, he was rector of Kingston Parish Church and then was transferred to Clarendon, where he served for 32 years. His first wife was [Smart] a daughter of Edward and Eliza Pennant, large landed proprietors in that parish. His second wife was Bathsuda, daughter of Florentius and Ann Vassal of the parish of St. Elizabeth. MAY PEN
>
> ...

Not all descriptions give as much as this introduction but I use it to illustrate the style of the book. Inez Sibley did extra research on Baptist churches and ministers, so if your ancestors were Baptist, and particularly missionaries, this book is a must. A copy of the book is in the FHLibrary at Salt Lake City. An older short article can be found in the RCS library: "Jamaican Place-Names" by F. Cundall (Kingston, 1909, 9 pp.).

A description of the historic buildings, sites and monuments of Jamaica was written by Frank Cundall in 1915: *Historic Jamaica* (London: West India Committee for the Institute of Jamaica. 1915. Reprinted, New York: Johnson Reprint Corporation, 1971, 424 pp.). The book is arranged by parish. A more recent publication with illustrations is *Jamaican Houses: a Vanishing Legacy*, text by Geoffrey de Sola Pinto with drawings by Anghelen Arrington Phillips (1982, Kingston, Jamaica: Stephensons Litho Press Ltd.).. The lithographs show not just several Great Houses of Jamaica, but houses such as a butcher shop and the railway station at Port Antonio, among 40 prints. I hear that this has been updated in a new edition but I cannot find out about it. Another book on Georgian houses is found in *Falmouth, 1793-1970*, published by the Georgian Society of Jamaica (Kingston, Jamaica: Georgian Society, 1970, 28 pp.). This book is illustrated with reproductions of old prints, photographs, sketches with street plans of Falmouth, and historical and architectural notes. Another look at Georgian architecture is given in "The Deceit of Motive: Looking back on the Georgian Age in Jamaica" by Alex Gradussov (*Jamaica Journal*, Vol. 5, No. 1, pp. 44-52, 1971).

An older work by Hakewill is used to illustrate many modern historical books of Jamaica: *A Picturesque tour of the Island of Jamaica, from drawings made in the years 1820 and 1821* by James Hakewill (London: Hurst & Robinson; E. Lloyd, 1825, 27 pp., 21 pp. of plates). This is a rare book. In the 1980s a similar set of plates was reproduced and sold as a set to the tourist trade. Most of the plates are of plantations and estates, many showing daily life before the end of slavery.

Another rare book used for illustrative purposes in modern books is *Daguerian Excursions in Jamaica, being a collection of views of the most striking scenery, public buildings and other interesting objects taken on the spot with the daguerrotype by Adolphe Duperly; and lithographed under his direction by the most eminent artists in Paris* (Kingston: published by A. Duperly, printed by Thierry Brothers, Paris, 1844 or 1850, 24 plates). John DeMercado has copies of these lithographs on his site at http://www.demercado.com/duperly.htm.

Two modern books about plantations include: *The Old Village and the Great House: an archaeological and historical examination of Drax Hall Plantation, St. Ann's Bay* by Douglas V. Armstrong (Illinois: Urbana University Press, 1990). The examination of Drax Hall from archeological expeditions throws light on how the slaves lived in the villages on an estate, at least as far as can be deduced from artifacts gathered at the site. The contrast is made to the occupants of the Great House whose artifacts were also catalogued. The second is *A Jamaican Plantation: the History of Worthy Park 1670-1970* by Michael Craton and James Walvin (Toronto: University of Toronto Press, 1970, 344 pp.) (see also History). The history of Worthy Park is drawn from estate books which have been preserved in large numbers. Some articles with pictures include: "The Oldest Jamaican Sugar Estate" by Michael Craton (*Jamaica Journal*, Vol. 4, No. 3, pp. 2-5, 1970), and "Kenilworth Ruins: a Note on Kenilworth, Maggoty Cove, Hanover" by T. A. L. Concannon (*Jamaica Journal*, Vol. 8, No. 1, pp. 21-22, 1974).

Martha Brae has also been excavated and the resulting book is *Martha Braes' Two Histories: European Expansion and Caribbean Culture Building in Jamaica* by Jean Besson. Kingston: Ian Randle Publishers 2002, 464 pp. ISBN 976-637-076-1

Another book about archeological sites is *Spanish and English Ruins in Jamaica with A brief history of that tropical paradise since it was discovered by Christopher Columbus, the Great Navigator, and settled by his son, Don Diego Colon in 1509 as Duke of Veragua* by William B. Goodwin. With maps, drawing, photographs and data never before published to illustrate the text. (Boston: Meador Publishing Co 1946 no index, 1895 foldout map endpiece, 239 pp.) This book has a site by site description mostly of the Spanish ruins.

Historic Jamaica from the Air by David Buisseret (Kingston, Jamaica: Ian Randle Pub. 1996, pp 150 ISBN 976-8100-64-8.) is a new edition. This second edition in addition to a history of Jamaica has many maps, historic prints of Hakewill and Kidd as well as aerial photographs of many locations that are described in the text. The history starts with the Taino and continues to the present day 20th century. Since there are two editions, this latter edition is able to contrast late 1960's aerial photographs with early 1990's pictures. Several old plantations houses and ruins are shown as well as aerial views of how the sugar estates and coffee plantations are/were laid out. Many views, ports and towns and bays are shown in beautiful colour photographs.

Photographs made in the 1890s of the countryside of Jamaica illustrate a book which was written to encourage tourists and others to visit the island and presented at the World's Fair (Columbian Exposition) in Chicago in 1893: *World's Fair: Jamaica at Chicago. An account descriptive of the colony of Jamaica, with historical and other appendices*, compiled under the direction of Lt. Col. the Hon. C. J. Ward, C.M.G. Honorary commissioner for Jamaica (New York: W. J. Pell, Printer, 1893, 95 pp.). Jamaica was quite well prepared for this exhibition because it had had its own Exhibition in 1891. This is described in "When Jamaica Welcomed the World: The Great Exhibition of 1891" by Karen Booth (*Jamaica Journal*, Vol. 18, No. 3, pp. 39-51, 1985).

Another collector's item is a series of postcards made from early photographs and tinted. They were advertised in the *Daily Gleaner*, a newspaper, in 1905 like this:

SEND POST CARDS TO YOUR FRIENDS ABROAD -- PICTORIAL POST CARDS

The Views set forth on these Cards are clean and bright, and are tastefully finished. They are well fitted to convey to friends abroad or in the island excellent impressions of scenery and life characteristic of much of the island. The following is a list of some of them:

- A Distant View of Kingston Harbour
- Near View of Constant Spring Hotel
- Distant View of Constant Spring Hotel
- Near View of Port Antonio
- View of Port Antonio Harbour
- A Family View, Kent Village, Bog Walk
- A Halt in the Fern Valley
- A Study in Black and White
- A Washing Scene, Near Old Harbour
- Bamboo Glade, Worthy Park
- Waterfall, Road to Newcastle
- Lych Gate, Half-Way-Tree
- Richmond Railway Station
- Barbecues for Drying
- Sugar and Rum
- A View near Newport
- Gordon Town
- Cane River Falls
- River Scene
- River Falls
- "Home Sweet Home"
- Native Wedding Party
- "A Corner in Pines"
- Brown's Town Market
- Going to Ground
- Mandeville Market
- Pimento, Coffee, etc.
- Mending our Ways
- Royal Palms, Spanish Town
- "en route" Newcastle, looking towards Kingston

Price 1d each, Coloured Views 2d each

An article on postcards is found in the *Jamaica Journal*, viz. "Some Early Jamaican Postcards, their Photographers and Publishers" by Glory Robertson (*Jamaica Journal*, Vol. 18, No. 1, pp. 13-22, 1985), which will attract those who have photographers and publishers in their ancestry. Stamps are of interest to those mailing postcards and the article "Three hundred years of Postal Service in Jamaica" by Stephen

Hopwood (*Jamaica Journal*, Vol. 5, No. 2&3, pp. 11-15) has many illustrations.

Specific Places

If your ancestors came from Port Royal, Clinton Black has written *Port Royal: A History and Guide, including Map for a Walking Tour of Port Royal* (1988, 2nd edition, Kingston, Jamaica, Institute of Jamaica Publications, 90 pp. with many pictures and maps, ISBN 976-8017-06-6). Many of the famous citizens of Port Royal are described. Another book is *Pirate Port: The Story of the Sunken City of Port Royal*. By Robert F. Marx (London: Pelham Books 1968. First published by The World Publishing company, USA, 1967. Extensively illustrated particularly of artifacts found under the sea. Index. 190 pp).

Additional aspects of architecture and special towns are found in "Our Architectural Heritage: Houses of the 18th and 19th Century with Special Reference to Spanish Town" by T. A. L. Concannon (*Jamaica Journal*, Vol. 4, No. 2, pp. 23-28, 1970); and "Houses of Jamaica" by T. A. L. Concannon (*Jamaica Journal*, Vol. 1, No. 1, 1967, Devon House, St. Andrew). An older history of Spanish Town is found in an article in the RCS library entitled "Old St. Jago" by G. F. Judah (57 pp., Kingston, 1896). Another article on Spanish Town is "History from the Earth: Archaeological excavations at Old King's House [Spanish Town]" by R. Duncan Mathewson (*Jamaica Journal*, Vol. 6, No. 1, pp. 3-11, 1972). Yet another article in this journal covers the present capital, "Early Kingston" by Wilma Williams (*Jamaica Journal*, Vol. 5, No. 2&3, pp. 3-8, 1971). Spanish Town is well represented because another book is *Spanish Town: The Old Capital* by Clinton Black (The University Press, Glasgow, 1960, 63pp). This short little book was commissioned by the St Catherine Parish council with the aid of Clinton Black who was the Archivist of the Island records. The two end pieces are maps, one of Jamaica and the other of Spanish Town itself. The book describes the history of the town, during the Spanish period and the British Period as well as Spanish Town today (1960). The author discusses the buildings in the Square, including the Old Record Office and Archives, the Court House and the old Kings House, as well as the Cathedral, the Barracks and the Spanish Town Baptist Church. It ends with some places of Interest Near Spanish Town including Ferry, Tom Cringles Cotton Tree (since deceased) and the Arawak Village which used to be a Museum (now closed), and Colbeck Castle. There are some very nice photographs of the town and other places mentioned in the book.

The latest book on Spanish Town is: *Gone is the Ancient Glory: Spanish Town, Jamaica 1534-2000* by James Robertson. Kingston: Ian Randle Publishers 2005, 498 pp ISBN 976-637-197-0.

Also "The Kingston Parish Church" by Marguerite Curtin (*Jamaica Journal*, Vol. 17, No. 4, 1985), and "The History of the St. Andrew Parish Church" (author Anonymous) in the *Jamaican Historical Society Bulletin* (Vol. 10, Nos. 1&2, pp. 309-329, 1989). In addition to the history, this article lists the clergymen who filled the role of rector to this parish church in Half-Way-Tree. Another article recalls "The History of Portland, 1723-1917", by B. Brown (*Jamaica Journal*, Vol. 9, No. 4, pp. 38-44, 1976). The latter was expanded to a book for use in elementary schools in the island, *A Short History of Portland* by Beryl M. Brown. (Jamaica: Ministry of Education Publications Branch, PO Box 498, Kingston, Jamaica 1976, 48 pp) It treats the Maroons in Portland, Sugar production in Portland, the Banana Trade and Tourism, the Rivers of Portland, including the Rio Grande and rafting. In "People and Places in Portland's history" it covers a few of the most famous places, including Manchioneal. On Machioneal it says,"This is now an important district in Portland. It was the scene of some adventures which Michael Scott wrote about in his story Tom Cringle's Log. At Muirton, there is an old great house to which Tom is said to have been taken when he landed from Cuba with yellow fever." The people it refers to are Thomas Clement Darlington Geddes and Frederick M. Jones. Lorenzo Dow Baker is pictured. There some nice black and white photographs, including one of Muriton Great House, and line drawings and three maps. The Falmouth Court House is described in *The History of the Falmouth Courthouse* by D. L. Ogilvie (privately printed in Falmouth, Jamaica, 1930, 49 pp.). Copy in the RCS library. An early description of St. Andrew is included in "The settlement of the Liguanea plain between 1655-1673." by W. A. Claypole (*Jamaica Historical Review*, Vol. 10, pp. 7-15, 1973). Copy in the RCS library.

Clinton Black has also written a history of Montego Bay. *The History of Montego Bay* by Clinton V. Black. (Montego Bay, Jamaica : Montego Bay Chamber of Commerce Printed in Kingston, United Co-operative Printers Ltd. 1984 , illustrations, coat of arms, index, brief bibliography, 56 pp.). The cover has the city coat of arms on it and it starts with Montego Bay in Spanish Times. It includes a section on Sam Sharp and the end of Slavery as well as the Rose Hall Story. Three pages are devoted to places of interest in the City, many of which are illustrated with photographs. I bought it on the used book market.

Vale Royal: the House and People by Enid Shields (Kingston, Jamaica: Jamaican Historical Society.1983 pp 74) details the history of a famous house. Vale Royal is a property in St Andrew that originally belonged to Col Henry Archbould 1669 or his relative James. In 1980 it became the home of the Prime Minister, the Edward Seaga. In between it was occupied by the Colonial secretaries 1929-1959, and from 1962 the Finance Ministers. Before it was sold to the Government in 1929, the home belonged to following families: Archbould, Lascelles,Lawes,Luttrell, Mitchell, Taylor, Bayley, Aikman, Gordon, Murray, Jackson, Scotland, Nuttall, Goegahan. There is a plan of the estate in 1813 and several pictures of the interior in 1983,some occupiers and their contemporaries. Some of the early families and the later occupants are described from sources in the archives and biographies. Sources are listed. Very interesting not only for those whose ancestors lived there, but also as an illustration of what can be found in the archives of deeds of houses and wills.

Land

During the Spanish occupation of Jamaica, the inhabitants mainly developed the southern parts of the island, clearing land of tropical forest to raise cattle and other livestock to sell to the Central American Spanish colonies. There were also settlements on the North Coast, but not very much in the interior of the island. Land records from this time, if they exist, must be in Spanish Archives. I have not done any investigation on this topic. The various "savannahs" denote areas which were cleared by the time the British conquered the island in 1655.

After the conquest, all land belonged to the government, and after 1660 to the crown. People who were recruited to colonize the island or those who emigrated there patented land from the crown. A copy of the **proclamation by Charles II in 1661** to recruit people to the island can be seen in the *Jamaica Journal* (Vol. 8, Nos. 2 & 3, p. 29, 1974). There was no freehold or copyhold land as had developed from the manorial system in England (at least it was not called that), although a yearly quit rent or land tax was collected by the government. The purported size limit of a land patent was 300 acres, but it is quite obvious that this was often ignored. One member of the Beckford family by 1754 had more than 22,000 acres.

After land was patented, it either passed down in the family to the heir (in wills, "real" property) or was sold by deed. If no heirs could be found for a patent, the land reverted to the crown, and future purchasers of the land had to pay a tax or escheat to the island treasury. During the first part of the 1700s the officials abused this custom, and complaints of the abuse were filed in England. Such a complaint was published as *The Groans of Jamaica, expressed in a Letter from a gentleman residing there, to His friend in London; containing a detection, and most convincing narrative of some of the crying grievances, and fraudulent oppressions, which give first Rise to the present growing Discontents, Divisions, and Animosities, among the Inhabitants of that Island: as also Particular Characters of the chief Authors and Promoters of these Distractions* (London, printed in the year 1714). This 48 page "letter" is interesting for its language and for a portrayal of the problems early land owners had.

Most of the crown lands had been patented by 1828, and thereafter expect only to find deeds of land transfer. After emancipation in 1834, many of the churches acquired defunct properties and estates, and divided the land up for former slaves. At this time smallholdings of two acres or less became common and the deed books increasingly large. Land settlements of divided government and private property have continued up to the latter part of the 20th century.

Patents

The documents generated by patenting land are interesting. One from 1740 is illustrated in part.

Volume 22, p. 5 Oliver Herring 19th March 1740

George II.
Whereas Colonel O. . . . H. . . . . has transported himself and servants and slaves in pursuance of the proclamation of the reign of Charles II to Jamaica to become one of our Planters, 300 acres of land, lying above Musketo Cove in the Parish of Hanover, including land, woods, easements, mines, minerals except gold and silver for the yearly rent of twelve shillings and sixpence (Jamaican money) to be paid on the Feast day of St. Michael and ... by even and equal portions and 1/20th of the yearly profits of all mines on the Feast day of St. Michael, the Archangel. ... Bear arms ... Provided within 3 years from the date he keep a number of white men proportionate to the number of slaves therein employed and keep white men on the land, pursuant to our instruction of 1st July 1735.

Signed by Edward Trelawny, Esquire, Captain.
(Governor)

Some points of interest: The preamble about "transporting himself" was not true in this case; his family had owned land (and he had lived in the island) in St. Elizabeth and Westmoreland since 1677, but not in Hanover parish. Even in 1740 the government expected to find gold and silver in Jamaica, and it would belong to the crown. Other mineral mines also were to profit the government. The patentee had to be willing to bear arms to protect the island from invasion, mainly the French and Spanish. And by the order of 1735, proprietors had to agree to employ a certain number of white men in proportion to the number of slaves they owned. The governor signed the patent. These records were enrolled in Spanish Town, the capital. Often a sketch of the property is included in the enrolled patent document. Although this is not to scale, the sketch often includes the names of people who held adjoining property which is useful in tracing families who married into the patentee's family. Some of the adjoining property was described as "unsurveyed", which I take to mean it was not yet patented. These patents while giving the parish do not reveal the name of the property, which must be sought in other family documents, if deeds of sale of the land are to be pursued.

In addition to land patents, patents were also taken out for naturalization of alien immigrants. The index references for naturalization patents which I have seen pertain mainly to Jews and French citizens, judging by the surnames. K. E. Ingram (*Sources of Jamaican History*, see before) also claims that the patent records include enrollment of credentials of (Church of England) clergy presented to livings in Jamaica in accordance with an act of 33 Charles II. I have not seen any references to these in the indexes I have examined.

Patents have not been microfilmed and the only sources currently are the RGO in Spanish Town, Jamaica (Ref 1B/11), and private family documents in record depositories. There are 43 volumes of patents including two index volumes in the RGO. They cover the period 1661 to 1828.

David Bromfield on his web page http://www. bromfield. us/ offers a service with Wayne Burnside to search patents and deeds in Spanish Town. You will find a description of the records that Wayne searches and the fees on David Bromfield's site. It is a fairly expensive search option but less than a trip to Jamaica! It is possible to negotiate the fees with Wayne via his e-mail address given on the site.

Deeds

Deeds, sometimes called Indentures, were made between people selling land, leasing land and selling slaves. I am not sure but I think also that marriage settlements (agreements drawn up before a marriage to protect the woman), especially if they involved land, were also enrolled as deeds. Deeds for land usually start off with listing the parties to the deed or indenture, e. g. George Lowe party of the first part to Mary Green party of the second part, and perhaps someone of the third part. Then the agreement is set out, signed by all parties and witnessed. An enrolled deed will also often tell when it was enrolled and attest to the authenticity of the signatures. Deeds therefore can reveal not only information about land transactions, but might also contain names of people related to the family or close neighbours. Often land deeds were quite long and covered all the contingencies if the grantor or grantee deceased before the transfer was accomplished.

Deeds for the sale of slaves were quite short as shown in the following example:

On the Recto:

Abraham Isaacs Esquire
Bought of Robert Robinson CCA
at Public Sale

August 10th 1832. A Negro man Slave named Allick, given u/v for Taxes due by John Lynch Reid Esq £35

> Received Payment
> R. Robinson CCA

Jamaica SS
    Before me personally appeared Robert Robinson Collecting Constable of Arears for the Parish of Saint Ann and acknowledged the signature of Robert Robinson with the Initials "CCA" set and subscribed to the above Bill of Parcel and receipt to be the proper handwriting of the said Robert Robinson.
Jas L Hilton

On the Verso:

I do swear that I have counted the words in the nether mentioned Instrument and find it to contain Legal Sheet 103 words to the best of my knowledge and belief.

H Melling Sn

Title for
a slave

Sworn before me this
13th of Nov 1833.
A Isaacs

Also:

Robinson R. CC
to
Isaacs, Abr

Entd 27 Nov 1833

Enrollment the Office of Enrollments
27 Nov 1833 Lib[er] 787, fol[io] 124

The above was the original deed and was entirely handwritten, but another I have of 1834 was printed with handwritten details filled in. All enrolled deeds would be copied into the liber by a clerk, so would not show the original signatures.

As shown above, there were at least two parties to the deed, the grantor and grantee. The Registrar General's Office at Spanish Town has indexes to both grantors and grantees for the deed books held in the RGO. Neither the indexes nor the deeds themselves have been filmed to my knowledge. The indexes give the liber, folio, year, To:, From:, and a short explanation e. g. Sale of Land, or Sale of Slaves. In later indexes on land the acreage is given, and you can trace sales of pieces of bigger estates by the name of the property if you know the parish.

There are more than 1,262 volumes or libers of deeds from 1664, including 61 index volumes (31 for grantors and 30 for grantees). There are actually two series of these deeds, one of 985 volumes and one of 216 volumes.

Wayne Burnside offers a service   to search deeds in Jamaica at Spanish Town Archives. He can be contacted through David

Bromfield's web page http://www. bromfield. us/ You will find a
description of the records that Wayne searches and the fees on David
Bromfield's site. It is a fairly expensive search option but less than a
trip to Jamaica.

Surveyors' Plans and Houses

Please refer to the chapter on Maps for more information on these
two aspects of land transfer. In particular, the Surveyor's Map collection
in the NLJ is of interest in this regard.
See also: Lists of Persons for Proprietors' lists.

Censuses and Lists of Persons

People in Jamaica have been counted since Britain conquered the island. However these records were mainly for statistical purposes, and it was very difficult to find out if original material from official censuses exists which might be of interest to the family historian. Counts of people are shown in the following table:

Year	No. of Whites	No. of Blacks	Total
1662	3,653	552	4,205
1673	7,768	9,504	17,272
1764		146,454 (Slaves)	166,454
1775	12,737	192,787 (Slaves) Free Coloured 4,093	209,617
1785*	30,000	250,000 Free Coloured 10,000	290,000
1807	—	—	319,351
1844	15,776	293,128	
		Coloured 68,529	
	English 3,450	Scots 1,523	
	Irish 1,298	Other British 1,689	
	French 1,342	Germans 615	
	Americans 480	Spaniards 331	
	South American 225	East Indian 1	
		African ** 33,519	377,433
1871	—	—	506,154

Year	No. of Whites	No. of Blacks	Total
1881	—	—	580,804
1889	14,692	488,624	
		Coloured 121,955	
	East Indian 10,166	Chinese 481	
		Colour not stated 3,623	
	Male 305,948	Female*** 333,543	639,491
1921	—	—	858,118
1943	12,310	965,944	
	Coloured 216,250	Jews 1,067	
	Chinese 6,894	Chinese Coloured 5,515	
	East Indian 21,396	East Indian Coloured 5,114	
	Syrian 835	Syrian Coloured 171	
		Other Races 1,327	1,237,063
1970	—	—	1,861,300

* Counts for the year 1785 must be estimates, since the numbers are rounded to three significant zeros.

** Of the total Coloured population this number were born in Africa. The rest were born in Jamaica.

*** Note the female population exceeds the male population.

Censuses

As far as I have been able to ascertain, a census was taken in each of the following years:

1844	1921 – 25th April
1861	1943 – January
1871	1960 – 7th April
1881	1970 – April
1889	1982
1911 – 3rd April	1991 & 2001

In one source the 1943 census was listed as the eighth census ever taken, thus confirming the number of censuses prior to that date. As mentioned before, there are compilations of statistical data taken from these censuses; the biggest collection of which I know, outside of Jamaica, is in the Smathers Latin American Collection in the Library of the University of Florida, Gainsville, FL. However, what family historians would like to have is the original data with families' names and locations if they exist in any form. And whether the schedules if they exist, list just household heads or include names of children and ages of all persons by parish. It seemed likely that the manner in which British census records were kept would be replicated in some form in Jamaica since it was a British colony, but that is not the case. As far as I have determined the early censuses schedules were not kept so there are no household data prior to 1970 to be found in Jamaica.

Lists of Persons

1670

The first available list that I know of is of 1670 in the source *Sketch Pedigrees of some of the early settlers in Jamaica* by Noel B. Livingston (Kingston, Jamaica: Educational Supply, 1909. Part IV. Microfilmed by the FHLibrary, Salt Lake City. FHL Catalog: Jamaica/Genealogy). The list is by parish of those parishes settled by 1670, and shows the number of acres patented by each landholder. Only males are listed. The list was signed by the Receiver General, Thomas Tothill, and was dated September 3, 1670.

1680

The National Archives (Kew, formerly the PRO) holds a list of the Inhabitants of Port Royal and St. John parishes in 1680 (1680 CO 1/45, ff. 96-109). Inhabitants of Port Royal and St. John only.

1655-1790

This list is known as *Official & Other Personages of Jamaica, From 1655 to 1790, to which is added, A chapter on the Peerage &c in Jamaica*, compiled from various sources by W. A. Feurtado (Kingston, Jamaica: W. A. Feurtado's & Sons, 1896, 130 pp.). Feurtado drew heavily on the records of the House of Assembly, so many people holding membership in the House are listed. Also military and naval personnel are included as official persons. Before the alphabetical list, there are several lists of very high officials, namely: a list of the Governors and Lt. Governors 1661-1895, Presidents of the Council 1661-1894, Speakers of the House of Assembly 1664-1863, Chief Justices 1677-1896, Attorneys General of Jamaica 1671-1896, Island Secretaries 1660-1872, Provost Marshalls General of Jamaica 1660-1872. After the body of the book the last section is devoted to showing how Jamaican families were related to British Peers. You need to take some care with this book and verify from original sources. Feurtado did make errors on dates and places. Pedigrees in the peerage section are incomplete. This list has been microfilmed in an obscure film of papers held by the National Library of Wales, Aberystwyth, containing notes, letters and pedigrees of the Ellis family who were prominent in Jamaica in the eighteenth century. Since the Ellis/Beckford Pedigree is contained in Feurtado's book, it was probably kept with these manuscripts as documentation. The film is indexed in the FHL Catalog under Jamaica/History and Jamaica/Genealogy. Patricia Jackson on her site has this list of persons.

1731-1868

A useful source for those who were considered ladies and gentlemen is *Gentleman's Magazine* which recorded births, deaths and marriages from 1731-1868. This *Magazine* has been extracted for North America and is available as *American Vital Records from the Gentleman's Magazine, 1731-1868* compiled by David Dobson (Baltimore: Genealogical Publishing Co., Inc., 1987, 310 pp., ISBN 0-8063-1177-0. Hardcover, typescript). In spite of the title, a large number of the entries are for people in Canada and the West Indies (including Jamaica, Barbados, Antigua and St. Kitts) rather than the United States. A typical death entry:

> BOURKE, John, b. 1776, late Kingston, Jamaica,
> d. Knightsbridge 20 Oct 1814.   (84:503)

The numbers in parenthesis represent the volume and page in the original *Magazine*. Take care with these numbers since there is also a New Series (NS) for some of the entries which leads to a different volume. Data should be carefully verified if taken from the Dobson book. I have noted some persons who were 125 years old at death, and even one of 145 years! I am sure in these cases there is a typographical error in one of the dates given.

The original *Gentleman's Magazine* can be consulted for additional information, since these are extracts, but there may be little additional information.

1717

The National Archives Kew, (formerly the PRO) holds a list for Spanish Town inhabitants in 1717 which includes nationality (CO 152/12, No 67 [vi]).

1754

A list of landholders who held more than 50 acres in 1754 was compiled and a typescript format is available in the National Library of Jamaica (Institute) (Call number NLJ F333.3 Ja Lis). The title is *A List of Landholders in the Island of Jamaica in 1754*. Its source "Received with Governor Knowles Letter Dated ye 31st December 1754. Taken from Quit Rent Books". The list includes the Landholder's Name, Number of Acres held and Locality (Parish). The name of the property is not given. The names are grouped by letters of the alphabet but are not alphabetical, so for example you have to search all the A's if your ancestor's name began with that letter. This appears to be because records are alphabetical by parish. Occasionally the landowner's name will be an estate, e.g. *William Gallimore, Estate*, meaning that the owner had deceased and the heir was not yet in possession I presume. This list also gives the following data which show the parishes with the most landowners in them:

Parish	Acres	Rank
Clarendon	230,688	1
St. Elizabeth	219,688	2
Westmoreland	161,175	3
St. Thomas Ye East	108,668	4
St. Mary	108,160	5
St. James	107,068	6
St. Andrew	102,143	7
St. Catherine	90,167	8
St. Ann	81,012	9

Very few women are listed since, in general, they did not hold land. Although free men of colour could have owned land at this time, the likelihood of their owning 50 acres or more is slim; therefore most people on this list will be white. They are also most likely to have been slaveholders.

An original copy of this list is to be found in the National Archives, Kew 1754 CO 142/31: *List of landholders with number of acres, taken from the Quit Rent Books*. This list has property holders with less than 50 acres as well as the larger land holders. A copy of this list is on Patricia Jackson's web site at: http://jamaicanfamilysearch.com/Samples2 /1754lead.htm. This is a members page. Also in the National Archives Kew is a list of St. Andrew's Parish (1753 CO 137/28, pp. 171-174. St. Andrew's Parish). This list shows plantation, landholder, numbers of acres, types of crops, livestock, number of slaves, etc. A copy of this was transcribed at: http://www.rootsweb.com/~jamwgw/1754andr.htm

1719-1825

Between these dates the Island Secretary sent a large number of lists to the Colonial Office, which are now housed in the National Archives Kew and listed in part in *Tracing your West Indian Ancestors* by Guy Grannum. These have been collected in CO 137/28 and CO 137/162 and include but are not limited to: Payments to Paupers; Slave Marriages in Portland, St. James, St. Catherine, Kingston and Manchester; Land grants 1735-1763 and 1805-1824; White families and Artificers, 1719-1732; Hanover Plantation names, owners; Manumission of Slaves, 1820-1825; Number and Names of Slaves sold for Taxes, 1821-1825; Portland Land grants; List of Vessels from the Coast of Guinea, 1752-1754.

1838

The *Jamaica Almanac* of 1838 (Appendix, pp. 160+) has a list of landowners by parish if the number of apprentices exceeds 20. Since this was the year of the end of Apprenticeship, this list gives the number of apprentices not slaves. An important aspect of this list is that the name of the property is given as well as the proprietor. The format is Parish, Proprietor Name, Property Name, and Number of Apprentices. The list is entitled *List of Proprietors and properties with the number of Apprentices where the number exceeds 20. As given in to the Parochial Vestries on 28 March, 1837.* A fair number of the proprietors are listed as deceased. A copy of this *Almanac* is available in the Rare Book Section of the Boston Public Library.
See also other Almanacs.

About 1907

In the National Library of Jamaica there is a one-volume manuscript which lists men born in Jamaica who matriculated at Oxford University in England. This volume was compiled by William Cowper, Headmaster of Jamaica College: *A catalogue of men born in the Island of Jamaica who matriculated at Oxford, 1689-1885 extracted from Alumni Oxonienses, by J. Foster, to which I have added some stray names of men connected with the Island* by William Cowper, MS 20, about 1907. There does not appear to be a comparable list from Cambridge University.

A list of all the Rhodes Scholars in Jamaica is available at:

http://www.rhodes-caribbean.com/register1.html from 1904 to the present. It has short bibliographies with the earlier scholars.

1912 and 1920

In the National Library of Jamaica (Institute of Jamaica) are also to be found two typescripts of proprietors (owners) and managers of properties in 1912 and 1920. These lists include, by parish, the name of the property, acreage, valuation in pounds, manager and use of the property, i.e. sugar cane, coffee, cattle pen, bananas, ruinate, small settlers, etc. Sometimes the owner and manager are the same person, especially if the property is small, but the addition of the manager's name on large properties enhances the extent of the lists. The source of these lists may be tax rolls, because the valuation is included. By comparing the 1912 and 1920 lists for the same property you may be able to narrow down a date for when a manager left employment and when a property passed from father to son or heir.

Twentieth Century

Lists of civil servants who served in Jamaica in the late 1800s and in the twentieth century may be found in the National Archives Kew reference room, CO 142, 1862-. You can find out more about this from Guy Grannum's book *Tracing your West Indian Ancestors*, Readers' Guide #11, 1995. Also the RCS library has the Jamaica Civil List revised to 30th November, 1926 (162 pp.).

Patricia Jackson on her web site http://jamaicanfamilysearch.com/ has lists of people which she has extracted from a varied number of sources some of which are described in this book.. As of June, 2006, the site has a number of persons exceeding 246,400 who were in Jamaica at least part of their lives. This site has a modest fee for signing up for 1 month, (in 2006 $8.00 US)

Ships' Passenger Lists

See under Immigration.

See also Lists of Slaves and Manumissions.

 # Immigration

The motto of Jamaica is "Out of many, one people". So it is no surprise that any family which has lived for generations in Jamaica will have a variety of countries to explore as the origin of their forebears. Because there are so many nations represented, I have not attempted to cover them all. If the country you are interested in is not represented in this section, do not assume that there is nothing available. I may simply not have come across any sources on the topic.

Ships' Passenger Lists – General

Many North Americans have a rich source in ships' passenger lists, particularly Filby, to verify the landing of their ancestors in the United States. Unfortunately, there are no comparable lists for Jamaica, at least none which I have been able to find. Perhaps, because Jamaica was a colony of Britain, the government did not deem it necessary to keep such data when British people arrived in Jamaica. And even the arrivals of people from other parts of Europe do not seem to have been deemed essential. The ships' passenger lists of Filby with updates do list some destinations as Barbados and other West Indian islands including Jamaica, so these lists are worth checking, but do not expect to find too much. Emigration **from** Britain by ship was only recorded beginning in the 1890s. (See also under England.)

Jamaica was not a penal colony so that unlike Australia, Barbados and the East Coast of the United States, searching in England for ancestors who were convicted of crimes and transported has in my experience been very unrewarding. In pursuing this line of research I noted that a few people transported had as their destination somewhere in the Caribbean, mostly Barbados or "Barbados or Jamaica", Nevis and Antigua. (See also under England.)

Jamaican landowners did employ "indentured white servants" from the 1660s to about the 1750s, but after the rise of the slave population this practice tapered off. There apparently are no lists of such people in Jamaica, although there are records of indentured servants traveling to America in which some West Indian servants are included. (See under England.) After they had served their time, they must either have blended in to the white population or some may have returned home. They are rather an elusive group because they are not listed by name in wills, as are many early slaves. Vital records of Jamaica do not identify them in any special way in christening, marriage or burial records. Many of course died of disease before their term of indenture expired, which may mean that they had no descendants.

Ships' lists of slaves were not kept.

In the Daily Gleaner newspaper there are some ships passenger lists beginning in the 1880's but these have not been indexed therefore you would have to know a year and approximate month to search these lists which appeared under The Harbour on page two of each issue. The Gleaner is now on-line. (See Newspapers) I was able to track my grandfather's arrival on the ship the RMS Don from Southampton, through Barbados and Jacmel (Haiti) to Jamaica until his arrival in Kingston in 1890 this way.

The Native People – Taino/Arawaks

When Christopher Columbus discovered Jamaica in 1494, the native peoples living there (I have seen estimates of 60,000) were the peaceful Indian group called the Taino, also called the Arawaks. These were in contrast to the fierce and warlike Caribs of the Eastern Caribbean. By the time the Spanish were ousted from the island in 1655, the Taino population was decimated by disease and overwork, for the Spaniards enslaved them. Thus it is extremely unlikely that you can trace any ancestors back to the Taino/Arawaks. I have seen one reference to a group of five slaves claiming to be free men because their forebears were "Indian". However I believe this is a reference to the Mosquito Indians from Central America who were brought to Jamaica, and not to the Taino. Nonetheless, the Taino are an interesting part of our history and it is enlightening to read what the island was like before Europeans and Africans inhabited the island. Some sources of their history and culture may be found in:

• *History of the Catholic Church in Jamaica* by Francis J. Osborne, S.J. (Chicago, Illinois: Loyola University Press, 1988, 532 pp.,

Chapter 1, LC BX1455.2.O84, IBSN 0-8294-0544-5). Father Osborne relied heavily on translated sources for this work. Observations by the Spaniards of the Taino/Arawaks are in Spanish Archives in Seville, and have not been translated often into English.

• *Origins of the Tainan culture, West Indies* by Sven Loven (Gotenberg, Sweden: Elanders Bockfryckeri Akfiebolag, 1935, 696 pp., 2nd edition, translated from Swedish). This includes Taino of West Indian islands besides Jamaica.

• *The Aborigines of Jamaica* by Philip M. Sherlock (Kingston: Institute of Jamaica, 1939, 20 pp. with map).

• *Columbus and the Golden World of the Island Arawaks* by D. J. R. Walker (Lewes, Sussex: The Book Guild Ltd., 1992, 320 pp., ISBN 086332686-2).

• "Christopher Columbus and the Treasure of the Taino Indians of Hispaniola" by Ricardo E. Alegria (*Jamaica Journal*, Vol. 18, No. 1, pp. 2-12, 1985, translated by James W. Lee). Although not Jamaican, the cultural objects described in this piece pertain to Taino Indians of Jamaica.

Africans

Accurately, African people did not immigrate to Jamaica since almost all were brought to Jamaica against their will as slaves. Emigration implies a degree of free will in the decision to move to another country, which choice they did not have. However since Africans are the largest group to influence the composition of the ancestry of the country, African roots will be addressed in this section.

We cannot all be as lucky as the American Alex Haley (author of the book *Roots*) who was able to trace his family back to a village in West Africa. For one thing, Haley had a very rich oral history that told him his roots were Mandingo and that Kunte Kinte had been "somebody" in his tribe. A second fact is that emancipation of slaves (1865) in America was one to two generations after emancipation in Jamaica (1834), thus there was more opportunity for the oral tradition which was handed down in Haley's family to be lost in a similar situation in Jamaica. Haley heard the stories from aunts who were children of slaves. A researcher today in Jamaica would have aunts who were three or more generations removed from the ancestor who was a slave. Once people are allowed to read and write, there is less pressure to preserve the oral tradition which is passed on from generation to generation in pre-literate societies. Even though importation of slaves was supposed to be abolished in the Southern states after 1808, many African slaves still entered the United States up to 1859, whereas the importation of slaves into Jamaica was abolished by British law in 1807. Not many were landed after this, and those who were captured in slave ships after this were handed over to the British Crown and often put into the military. Thus the chances of finding from oral history how and when one's African ancestors entered Jamaica are even less likely than in the United States.

There is also the barrier of what records are available. American records are different from Jamaican records for slaveholders. Some are better, some are less extensive. On the other hand, the sources available between 1834 and 1880 are better in Jamaica. Since many slaves and apprentices were baptized in the Anglican Church even as adults beginning in 1834, the vital records covering this period are a valuable resource not available to most African Americans in the same time period. In Jamaica, for some freed people of colour and even for a few slaves, the vital records can take one back to the 1750s, if one is lucky.

In a similar fashion to African Americans who search for their roots in America, one must be prepared to research the family history of the white families who owned the Jamaican ancestors. However reluctant one might be to spend time on people who degraded and enslaved other people, this is where the records are likely to be. Besides, not only may a white owner or one of his relatives be an ancestor, but his white overseers or book keepers may also turn out to be related. Those white ancestors are not any less important to diligent students of family history. We have to take our ancestors as we find them. Throwing them out or ignoring them is not going to make them go away as our ancestors.

With this said, a caution is in order. While you may be able to find your African family ancestors in Jamaica back to the 1830s with some assurance, you will begin to lose several lines at this time, because of the lack of records. Most Europeans lose lines in the 1600s for the same reason. Not being able to find records is one aspect that frustrates beginners in genealogy; knowing that there are no records to find is frustrating even to the most seasoned researchers.

Maroons

The maroons of Jamaica have been a topic of great interest, therefore several books have been written about them (see History section). I have found the book by Mavis Campbell to be one of the most readable: *The Maroons of Jamaica, 1655-1796: a history of resistance, collaboration & betrayal* by Mavis C. Campbell (Granby, Mass: Bergain

& Garvey, 1988, 296 pp.). Not only are the maroons of interest in themselves, but because of the two Maroon Wars they influenced the settlement of the island and brought British military units to the island. The first maroons were the slaves of the Spaniards who escaped when the British conquered the island in 1655 and hid out in the sparsely inhabited interior. They were joined over the years by runaway slaves eluding efforts to recapture them until the end of the first Maroon War, when the two main bands of maroons in Portland (Nanny town) and St. Elizabeth (Accompong) made a treaty with the British to return runaway slaves to the properties in return for peace (1740). Relative peace reigned for more than 50 years during which large areas were developed in sugar cane. But the new white settlers kept pushing back the enclaves of the maroons and encroaching the terms of the treaty, which resulted in the second Maroon War in 1795. Two articles which might be of interest are: "The Windward Maroons after the Peace Treaty" by Beverley Cary (*Jamaica Journal*, Vol. 4, No. 4, pp. 19-22, 1970), and "The Origin of the Second Maroon War, 1795-1796: A planter's Conspiracy?" (*Jamaica Journal*, Vol. 6, No. 1, pp. 21-25, 1972).

At the end of the second war, many maroons were transported to Nova Scotia, Canada, and finally to Sierra Leone in Africa. Some maroons remained in the island in isolation and up to this day are not as integrated into the society as others. Mavis Campbell describes oral interviews which she had with some of the descendants.

The Anglican vital records of Jamaica reflect the concentrations of maroons, and the parishes of Portland and St. Elizabeth have many records of baptisms (with change of names and addition of surnames) of people who were maroons. These records begin in about 1834 with the abolition of slavery. If you are going to find maroon ancestors, it is most likely if your recent ancestors came from these two parishes.

The National Archives, Kew (formerly the PRO), London, also holds some records of maroons in 1831; this includes name, age, also in some records colour, and return of slaves belonging to the maroons (*Return of Maroons of Moore Town, Charlestown, Scot's Hall and Accompong*, CO 140/121, pp. 353-378). There is also under Sierra Leone a *Return of Nova Scotians and Maroons* in 1802 (WO 1/352).

Slaves

After you have exhausted Civil Registration and church records for clues on the origins of your forebears, a book which may be helpful in tracing your African ancestors is *Slave Genealogy: A Research Guide with Case Studies* by David H. Streets (Bowie, Md.: Heritage Books Inc.,

1986, 90 pp.). It is however written for African-Americans, so that records which are illustrated by the author may not be available for the Jamaican. A more helpful book is *Searching for the Invisible Man: Slaves and Plantation Life in Jamaica* by Michael Craton with the assistance of Garry Greenland (Cambridge, Mass.: Harvard University Press, 1978, 439 pp.). This book traces the genealogy of several slave families, coloured slaves and whites from the records of Worthy Park, a sugar estate in Lluidas Vale now in St. Catherine, then in St. John's Parish. (See also under History for another book on Worthy Park.) This book shows what can be done when extensive plantation records are available for an estate; Worthy Park slave (and apprentice) lists exist for 1730 and then from 1784-1838. Also there are labourers' wages lists 1840-46. Add to this church records from St. John's Parish and slave lists available in the Registrar General's Office and the National Archives T71, and the authors are able to give some detailed pedigrees for a few slaves. They add from analysis and general history, pictures (snapshots really) of the lives of field hands, specialist slaves (coopers, masons, wainmen, etc.) and domestics using actual persons who were on the estate as examples. This is a good book to form a basis for family history of the ancestors, however it is the history of a large sugar estate which at its peak had more than 500 slaves. To give a comparison, Craton shows in Table 5 (p. 38) that in 1828 in Jamaica only 34 estates had a number exceeding 400 slaves, 107 with 300+ slaves, 277 with 200+ slaves, 614 with 100+ slaves, 560 with 50+ slaves and 641 with 25+ slaves. Thus Worthy Park represented about 1.5% of the estates in the size of its slave population. Estates with 25-50 slaves represented 53.8% of the estates and the lives of such slaves are more realistically described by Prof. Hall's *In Miserable Slavery* (see History). The latter book, which is essentially a transcription of a diary of plantation overseer and eventual owner Thomas Thistlewood, does not attempt as does Craton's *Invisible Man* to describe the genealogy of the slaves nor give an analysis of the demographics and daily work, but does give a graphic picture of day to day life on a small plantation which was devoted to raising provisions. Thistlewood never had more than about 30 slaves and also was a great experimenter, importing all sorts of seeds and plants from England to try out on his estate. His slaves moved more frequently off the plantation (with passes/tickets) than those at Worthy Park where only the wainmen appeared to have permission to travel. Anyone whose ancestors were raised in Lluidas Vale should consult the *Invisible Man* book, because there is a list given (Table 52, pp. 296-304) of people employed at Worthy Park from 1842-46 which gives their former slave names as well as their current names, occupations and birth dates. There are actually very few estate records that are as complete as those for Worthy Park which now exist, so while it is possible that Ingram's book *Sources of Jamaican History* (see History) can lead you to some manuscript records, do not expect to find comparable or as extensive records as those for Worthy Park.

Two additional books on late eighteenth and early nineteenth century slaves, of the many that have been written, include: *Slave Population and Economy in Jamaica, 1807-1834* by B. W. Higman (Cambridge: Cambridge University Press, 1976, pp. 327, ISBN 0-521-21053-4). There are a few genealogies given in this book (figure 30); they do not show names, but in two cases show a tracing through four generations. The second book which deals with a similar period is: *The Development of the Creole Society in Jamaica, 1770-1820* by E. Braithwaite (Oxford: Clarendon Press, 1971, 374 pp.). This book has an excellent section on practices at birth, marriage and death and burial, which were legacies of African practices. The thesis of this book is that both blacks and whites were Creolized or adapted to the slave society, and that the society that developed in Jamaica had significant influences on both of the major groups. The author also treats the free coloured people and institutions of the whites including: descriptions of the legislature, Assembly, slave laws, courts of law, vestries, the Anglican church, militias and the press. He also has gathered together from manuscript sources, mostly missionary letters, some interesting insights into what the slaves thought, e.g. about marriage, some poetry and song. This is difficult to ascertain because there are so few direct written records of what slaves felt or thought about their condition. Usually such passages are interpretations by white historians of how they thought the slaves felt.

Another book is *Slaves and Missionaries: The Disintegration of Jamaican Slave Society, 1787-1834* by Mary Turner Kingston, Jamaica: The Press University of the West Indies, 1998, pp 223. Paperback, ISBN 976-640-045-8.Previously published Urbana, Illinois: University of Illinois Press 1982. The paperback edition of this book has seven chapters. The first two chapters describe firstly the status and mind-set of the non-conformist men (ie. not Church of England/Anglican/Episcopalian) who went to Jamaica as missionaries and secondly, the status of slaves and briefly their religious beliefs drawn from Africa. The next two chapters describe how the missionaries interacted with the slaves and how this interaction influenced the process which led to emancipation. The influence of the Missionary societies on the antislavery politic is explained. The fifth chapter uses the Methodist missionary experience to show how religion influenced the slaves in their fight for freedom and the sixth chapter describes the period of 1831-1834 using the Baptist missionaries role in the largest Rebellion (1831) of that time. Sam Sharpe the National Hero is discussed briefly. The last chapter describes how freedom was actually achieved. If you have Methodist or Baptist missionaries or slave ancestors of the period 1823-34 this is a very compelling book. Although the title suggests a longer time period the meat of the book concentrates on the last decade before emancipation. The parts of the island referred to in more depth include St Ann, Trelawny and St James and Hanover etc., that is the County of Cornwall and St Ann from Middlesex. There are two maps, one of the Mission stations in 1834 and the second of the estates involved in the 1831 Slave Rebellion. There are many footnotes and an excellent bibliography. There are no illustrations except for the cover which is a reprint of a Duperly print of the Attack of the Rebels on Old Montpelier in 1831.

Some of the slave rebellions have been chronicled in the *Jamaica Journal*. These sources include: "Tacky and the great slave rebellion of 1760" by C. Roy Reynolds (*Jamaica Journal*, Vol. 6, No. 2, pp. 5-8, 1972) and "The Slave Rebellion of 1831" by Mary Reckord (*Jamaica Journal*, Vol. 3, No. 2, pp. 25-31, 1969).

Slave Names

It is generally understood that slaves did not have surnames and their forenames were given to them by their masters. It is said that this was because they were regarded as chattel of their masters and on an equal footing with the cattle and horses of the estate. However there is a documented exception that I have found in Jamaica in 1825 and it is not unique. This is chronicled in an article called "A Report on Excavations at Montpelier and Roehampton" by Dr. Barry Higman (*Jamaica Journal*, Vol. 8, Nos. 2 & 3, pp. 40-45, 1974). In this article an excerpt from an account book at Old Montpelier which is held by the Institute of Jamaica lists thirteen Negro houses where the inhabitants identified were families and dependents if any. All the slaves in this list had surnames; e.g., William Miller, Catherine Ellis, William Smart, Thos. Stewart Miller lived in "A good new House, boarded, Spanish walled and shingled; Kitchen and Hogsty". They had a total of 2 horned stock, 4 hogs and 11 poultry. The article is really an account of excavations at the estates for the Negro houses, and those estates were chosen because there was documented evidence of habitation. I have come across other excerpts in books on slavery where a surname was listed for a slave. There is also some evidence in the use of African names that Africans sometimes retained their forenames, probably more likely if no one else on the estate already had that name. After emancipation surnames become more controversial.

First, not all slaves took surnames (as seen from the records of Worthy Park), and they died with only one name. If however they were baptized in the established or non-conformist church, they almost always took surnames. It is obvious from the Anglican records that many did take the last names of the owners at the time of emancipation. So for example, you have a slave Priscilla taking the name Mary Crawford on Samuel Crawford's estate. However these records also reveal that of the many slaves on a particular plantation, a large proportion of them assumed surnames other than that of the owner. One error is to leap to the conclusion that they must have been sold from another plantation where they were born, and thus took the name from *that* estate owner. While this may be the case (infrequently I have found; after 1807 there were laws passed against the separation of family groups), other possibilities should be considered.

One such possibility is that they were descendants of an overseer or book keeper on the same estate. As seen above, on large estates many book keepers and an overseer were employed and they changed frequently. So that mulatto and quadroon slaves and ex-slaves were frequently the offspring of whites who had once been on the estate. If a mulatto or quadroon had children with an African, his offspring could have been designated a sambo and taken the surname of his grandfather. This means that more digging is required into the names and lives of the white employees of the estate. Yet another possibility is that the surname came from an earlier owner of the property on which the slave was emancipated. Since properties including slaves did change hands on the death of an owner, the forebears of the slave could have been a slave on the property at the time of the previous owner and assumed his name.

Another possibility is given in the book of Thistlewood of a small estate. Thistlewood encouraged some of his slaves to breed and increase by sending them to cohabit briefly on adjoining estates over which he had some influence. If you accept that Thistlewood had some idea of animal husbandry which he practiced on his own livestock to avoid excessive inbreeding, you can accept that he had some rationale for doing this with people that he regarded in the same light as cattle. Thus some ex-slaves may very well have known who their fathers were from an adjoining estate and taken their surnames at emancipation. When therefore you find a baptized slave from one estate having the surname of the owner of a nearby estate, it may not mean that they were sold off the latter estate. It also is obvious that learning the names of owners of adjoining estates is one way in which you might determine the origin of your ancestor's surname, if not his or her parentage.

Another possibility is that the ex-slaves took the last name of the curate or minister who baptized them, so pay attention to the officiating minister as you read the Anglican baptisms of the time of emancipation.

For first names there is quite a bit to be noted. Some African slaves had African names like the names given to denote the day they were born on, e.g. "Cubba" etc. (See General References.)   This can sometimes give a clue as to the likely tribe in Africa, but not always. "Betty's Jack" does give you a clue as to who Jack's mother was so you may be able to identify a further ancestor. Many slaves must have hated their given names, because when they selected names at baptism, they often changed from quite pretty or distinguished names (by today's standards) such as Daniel and Cindy to ordinary names like Mary and John. Names such as Strumpet and Whore (names on Worthy Park) I think anyone would have gotten rid of immediately. A full list of Worthy Park slaves in 1789 is given in an appendix of Braithwaite, *The Development of the Creole Society in Jamaica, 1770-1820.*

I noted in a series of inventories of wills starting in 1689 that the owners had given slaves the first names of their own Puritan ancestors and distant relatives but not those of the nuclear family of the estate. Also at this time, the names of Greek and Roman gods as well as biblical names were popular. By 1727 on the same estate, African names were more common but still not the predominant naming pattern. I hope to find later inventories which will tell how this progressed on the same estate towards emancipation.

Ships

The slaves were brought to the West Indies from West Africa in what is known as the Middle Passage, a trip of several months. This was because the ships left England (Bristol, Plymouth, Liverpool and London) with goods for trade in West Africa, picked up slaves to be brought to the West Indies and in a triangle returned to England with sugar, tobacco and rum from the Islands. Some of the descriptions of these voyages are well-documented in history books. An example is: *The Slave Trade: The History of the Atlantic Slave Trade: 1440-1870* by *Hugh Thomas*, (New York, Simon and Schuster, 1997, 926pp). Some additional data may be available in the initial ports. For example, the

Bristol record office has original papers from slave traders which are described in Leaflet #4 "Records relating to Slavery" (1994, 15 pp.). The leaflet states that between 1698 and 1807, "it has been calculated about 2,108 slaving ventures were fitted out in Bristol and about half a million Negroes transported across the Atlantic in Bristol ships". It is pointed out that Liverpool and London probably had a larger share of the trade, except for 1713-1730 when Bristol was the leading port. Records of the anti-slavery campaign are also held and this pamphlet includes a picture of how the lower deck of a slave ship was packed with slaves in the Middle Passage.

A fair idea of where the slaves came from in West Africa can be gained from a list of 241 African slaves in 1778 from York Estate, Trelawny (Gale-Morant Papers, University Library, Exeter, Devon, England). Slaves are listed in descending frequency of tribal labels: Eboe, Coromantee, Papa, Congo, Moco, Portage, Chamba, Fantee, Nago, Mandingo, Ashantee, Duccosia, Alio. Coromantee were regarded at first by the estate owners as good workers and desirable slaves, but when they proved rebellious and warlike were abandoned for the more placid Congo. So it depends what period you are researching for the most likely area for identification.

Newspapers

When ships came into the West Indies, auctions were held of the slaves and notices of these can be seen in newspapers of the day. The *Royal Gazette* and other advertizing sheets which are held in the NLJ (see section on Newspapers) can be consulted to find out how this was done, but this will not identify who bought the slaves or what their names were. If however you have identified when a plantation owner increased his slaves by purchase from Africa, you may be able to search the relevant newspapers for when and by what ship they arrived and the name of the slave merchant.

Newspapers which also had notices for runaway slaves and descriptions of the slaves or listed the plantation from which they escaped may be available. Some of these runaways ended up in the workhouse (poorhouse) of a parish and were auctioned off if their owners did not claim them. This is where I first came across the (shocking to me) fact that freed black people owned slaves. Such a runaway slave in a workhouse in St. James was described as owned by a free black woman. If not claimed by such and such a date ... the slave would be put up for auction.

Wills / Inventories / Deeds

Wills, inventories and deeds for the plantation owner can be searched for names of slaves. Plantation owners often manumitted some slaves in their **wills**. However these were most likely to be personal servants and house slaves, not field slaves. The major exception to this seems to have been field slaves with high skills, such as the masons, carpenters, coopers and still house keepers. The main group of slaves freed in a will was the owner's own sons and daughters by African, mulatto and mestee (mustee) slaves, along with their mothers. **Inventories** to wills, especially in the early years, often listed all the slaves on a plantation by name. If you are able to obtain a series of inventories you may be able to trace the progression of a slave through childhood to old age. I doubt however that estates with 400+ slaves would have had inventories with this amount of detail. **Deeds** were needed for the sale or acquisition of slaves. Sometimes the new slaves were acquired for a child of the owner, so look for deeds at the time that the owner's children were reaching the age of 18 years of age.

Manumission

As mentioned above, the term given to freeing of slaves was "manumission". This most often occurred at the death of the slave owner, but could also occur at other times. In the *Invisible Man*, Craton documents that at a large plantation like Worthy Park, in 1794-1837 a maximum of about two slaves per year were manumitted, and in some years none. Slaves may have been manumitted in a will as noted above; it was also possible that some slaves bought their freedom or that a freed person bought freedom for their kin. The main way slaves earned money to buy their freedom was by working the provision grounds and selling them in the market. It must have been strenuous to work all day and tend provisions which were often a good way off and then to harvest and sell them on the day set aside for rest, but the determined did it.

I also found it interesting that Thistlewood (mentioned above), who was intimate with a number of his female slaves, carefully noted in his diary what he paid his slaves for their coerced participation. Although the payment was minimal it was another way for female slaves to save money for their freedom. As an aside, I think that the necessity of the white owners to provide provision grounds to slaves (because they could not rely on the ships coming in on time to provide staple foods) set Jamaican and other West Indian island slaves up at emancipation. They had had the experience of being small entrepreneurs in provisions, and thus took to small holding and higgling more easily than those in America who had not had this opportunity.

The RGO in Spanish Town has lists of **manumitted slaves** from 1747 to 1838 included in 66 volumes with two index volumes (Ref 1 B/11). The enrolled manumissions are listed by the names of owners, then the names of slaves and how they obtained the manumission, i.e. by gift of the owner or by purchase. A few early volumes prior to 1747 are missing and so is Volume 30, 1804. The last volume, 1834/38, is actually manumission of apprentices, not slaves. These records have not been microfilmed to my knowledge.

A few individual manumissions are listed in family papers which are now in archives in England and held in Jamaica. You can search using the word "manumission" in the index of Ingram's book *Sources of Jamaican History* for these releases. Some limited manumission records of Jamaica are also to be found in the National Archives, Kew (TNA) Colonial Office series. See Grannum Guy, *Tracing Your West Indian Ancestors* (PRO Readers' Guide No. 11, 2nd Edition, 2002). Edward Crawford kindly sent me transcription copies of manumissions in CO 137/162 from TNA, Kew which are to be found on the World GenWeb Jamaica site at: http://www.rootsweb.com/~jamwgw/manum.htm . Some manumissions are also listed on Patricia Jackson's site.

Lists of Slaves

In 1807 the importation of slaves into Jamaica was prohibited by an act of Parliament. Because of this act, beginning in 1817 slave owners had to report the number of slaves they had and keep records of the yearly increase (by births) and decrease (by deaths) that occurred on their estates. (They also had a self interest in making it possible for births to occur by slightly easing the work of pregnant women, for there was no other source of new slaves.) This government requirement resulted in triennial lists known as Slaves Returns which are now in the Registrar General's Office at Spanish Town. There are 141 volumes (Ref 1B/11), and they cover the period 1817 to 1832. A register includes a parish or group of parishes, and includes an index by the names of owners or trustees to an estate. The slaves are listed under owner by sex, given names, colour, age, whether African or Creole, and can include remarks such as if the slave was the son or daughter of another slave. This list is a treasure trove if you know the owner or estate of the ancestor. However, even if you know the parish, it may be a place to start. These records have not been microfilmed to my knowledge. In England, a Registry of

Slaves is found in the National Archives, Kew in class T71 which I have examined for limited parishes.

An example is given taken from T71/43 for 1817 from the Parish of St Ann:

Jamaica SS

A return of slaves in the parish of Saint Ann in the possession of **Charles Dussard** as Natural Guardian of **Charles Samuel Dussard, Benjamin Henry Dussard, and Lydia Augusta Dussard** his sons and daughter the owners on the 28th Day of June in the year of our Lord 1817.

Names Names of all males to precede the names of females	Colour	Age	African or Creole	Remarks
Males				
James	Negroe	32	African	
Dick	Negroe	20	African	
Neptune	Negroe	2	Creole	Son of Sophia
Females				
Sophia	Negroe	21	African	
Eliza	Negroe	18	African	

Males 3 Three
Females 2 Two
Total 5 Five

I **Charles Dussard** do swear that the above list and return consisting of one sheet is a true prefect and complete list and return to the best of my knowledge and belief in every particular therein mentioned of all and every slave and slaves possessed by me as Natural Guardian of three of my children above names the owners considered as most permanently settled worked or employed in the parish of Saint Ann on the twenty eighth day of June one thousand eight hundred and seventeen without fraud, deceit or evasion

Sworn before me this twenty fifth   So help me God
Day of September one thousand eight   *Charles Dussard*
Hundred and seventeen   *John Chrystie*

Slavery was abolished August 1, 1834. Newspaper accounts of the celebration of that day can be seen in the 1955 *Daily Gleaner* and other historical sources. A little-known fact is that the Jewish Rothschild family gave the British government 20 million pounds to reimburse planters for the loss of their worth which was tied up in slaves. Without this donation, the emancipation would have been further delayed.

Some French slaves entered the island in the late 1790s with their masters from Haiti; however, unless they are listed in the above lists later in the nineteenth century or there are will inventories from their masters, it may not be possible to identify them.

Apprentices

After emancipation in 1834, ex-slaves were known as apprentices. The idea was that for six years they would learn the arts of citizenship, and become educated and Christians, after which they would be full citizens. It was a dismal failure. The former owners were bitter and often treated their ex-slaves more harshly than previously, turning them off the land with nowhere to go. They paid them non-living wages for the work on the estates. The non-conformist religionists tried to help by buying up ruinate land and parceling it out to the people so that they could make a living. Of course the slaves preferred this freedom to determine their own destiny and refused to work on the plantations even for a wage. Many estates failed. This made the plantation owners even more bitter and revengeful against the religionists. In the established church, most of the Anglican clergy took the part of the plantation owners, although they were supposed to be setting up schools and giving religious instruction to the ex-slaves. The Anglican parish baptism and marriage records do record from 1834-38 a large number of "apprentices", no doubt so ordered to do by the Bishop of Jamaica. At baptism apprentices often changed their names from their slave names, however there is much less a tendency to record their former name when they were apprentices in the period 1834-38 than prior to that time. Apart from these parish records, I know of no lists which would give the names of apprentices. There should be non-conformist records but few of them seem to have been publicly deposited. If you can find land records of deeds to land supplied to the newly freed people at this time, this may in specific areas give you some clues.

Apprenticeship was such a dismal failure that it was ended two years early, and ex-slaves gained full freedom in 1838. A book which deals with emancipation and apprenticeship in Jamaica is W. L. Burn, *Emancipation and apprenticeship in the British West Indies* (London: Jonathan Cape, 1937. Reprinted New York, London: Johnson Reprint Corporation, 1970, 398 pp.). An article in the *Jamaica Journal* also deals with the apprenticeship period: "Not 'Full Free': The ex-Slaves and the

Apprenticeship System in Jamaica 1834-1838" by Swithin Wilmot (*Jamaica Journal*, Vol. 17, No. 3, pp. 2-10, 1984). Emancipation on a particular estate seems to have occurred prior to general emancipation and a short account is available in the RCS library entitled: *An Account of the emancipation of the Slaves of Unity Valley Pen in Jamaica* (20 pp., 1801) by D. Barclay.

Free Coloured People

In 1775 the census records that there were 4,093 free coloured people, and in 1785 a rough estimate was that there were 10,000 free coloured people. These numbers are very hard to verify. As seen above, freedom was obtained through manumission especially at the time of death of a former owner, i.e. by will. Many of the pre-1834 records of vital records of free persons can be found in parish records, where they were designated as free black man, or free mulatto woman, etc. Other records of these people are hard to find; they did not have rights as did people who were born white. They probably did not own extensive property, so are not in lists of property owners of greater than 50 acres, but some deeds probably exist although they would be difficult to distinguish. I have noticed in the Jamaica Almanacs some designations of "fp" after a name which must mean "free person" but this is not frequent. Many but not all of the free people were of mixed race. Free people mainly engaged as merchants, for example as tavern owners or shopkeepers, and probably some earned their living by hiring out small numbers of jobbing slaves prior to the end of slavery. Jobbing slaves were slaves for hire at peak cane season, who might also be hired to a vestry to repair roads and other parish works.

A free person, to aspire to the status of society of the time, needed to have slaves and also to be a Christian. These free persons later became the backbone of the Jamaican middle-class and several histories have examined the rise of this group. For example: Mavis C. Campbell, *The dynamics of change in a slave society: a sociopolitical history of the free coloreds of Jamaica, 1800-1865* (Rutherford, New Jersey: Fairleigh Dickinson University Press, 1976, 393 pp.), and G. J. Heuman, *Between black and white: race, politics and the free coloreds in Jamaica, 1792-1865* (Westport, Connecticut: Greenwood Press, 1981, 231 pp.).

Another book already mentioned which deals with such topics is: *The Development of the Creole Society in Jamaica, 1770-1820* by E. Braithwaite (Oxford: Clarendon Press, 1971, 374 pp.). Similar attributes are discovered in R. T. Smith, *Kinship and class in the West Indies: a genealogical study of Jamaica and Guyana* (Cambridge University Press, 1988, 205 pp.).

African Labourers 1840-1865

A little-known aspect of Jamaican history is that after the abolition of slavery and apprenticeship, there were attempts made to recruit paid labourers from Africa. While the numbers who came were not large (estimated 10,000) compared to slaves, your Jamaican ancestors may never have been slaves. A book on this topic has been published by the Institute of Jamaica and republished by the University Presses of Florida. The full reference is: Mary Elizabeth Thomas, *Jamaica and voluntary laborers from Africa, 1840-1865* (Gainsville: University Presses of Florida, 1974, 211 pp., ISBN 0813004381). A review of this book is given in an article in the *Jamaica Journal*: "The Last Africans: a review Article" by H. P. Jacobs (*Jamaica Journal*, Vol. 8, No. 4, pp. 32-35, 1974).

There were also suggestions that Jamaica recruit free blacks from America, however this proved very difficult, so it is not possible to know how many did come. A few free black Americans were some of the first Baptist lay-preachers in the island. (See under Baptists)

The *Jamaica Journal* also has an interesting article on Afro-Jamaican beliefs and rituals associated with death and burial: "A Note on Afro-Jamaican Beliefs and Rituals" by Elizabeth Pigou (*Jamaica Journal*, Vol. 20, No. 2, pp. 23-26, 1987), which describes slave funerals and Kumina funeral rituals.

The Daily Gleaner on-line has a series called Pieces in the Past. Included are a section called Out of Many Cultures, The People who came. In this section are The Africans at:
http://www.jamaica-gleaner.com/pages/history/story0059.htm

American Loyalists

If you are having trouble tracing an ancestor from Jamaica back to the United Kingdom, you might consider the possibility that the family at one time resided in America prior to the American Revolution.

At the time of the American Revolution (1775-1782), it was estimated that 30 percent of the populace was loyal to England and to the king. After the Revolutionary War ended, many of these loyalists fled to Canada, especially to Nova Scotia, and some returned to Britain. A small number of loyalists went to Jamaica, and of these many settled on land in St. Elizabeth. They are not usually to be found in books on American loyalists (at least I have not yet found any), based on their claims for compensation of the losses they incurred, but scattered records do exist. For example a list of the names of 183 heads of loyalist families who emigrated from Charleston, South Carolina, in December 1782 to Jamaica, is in the Hunt MSS U.I. 14, Vol. 1, Nos. 19-20 in the Boston Public Library. There is also a list of loyalists in the *Journal of the House of Assembly* in Jamaica (1784 25 George III P 37) when the government was appealed to in order to assist the new arrivals, and a list of loyalist certificates compiled by George F. Judah (MS #1841, Institute of Jamaica). The latter two lists have been microfilmed (called "Loyalists who fled to Jamaica after the American Revolution") from a manuscript donated by Carolee Mitchell, Brooklyn NY (6 leaves), by the LDS Church and can be found in the British film area FHL Catalog film #0994065, item 3. Some of the loyalists returned to America and some of their correspondence to relatives remaining in America from Jamaica exists. See Ingram's *Sources of Jamaican History* for manuscript locations.

Some slaves also came with the white loyalists from the United States at this time, but they are not likely to be listed in the above sources.

English

The early English Settlers

After the conquest of Jamaica, some of the former soldiers who came with Penn and Venables were encouraged to settle down and become landowners and farm. Many were not very good at this occupation and their health in the new country was so poor that many died. *Caribbeana*, Volume 2, p. 251 has "A particular list of persons paid their first months pay for their respective qualities under the command of General Venables, December, 1654". Most of these early settlers developed former land occupied by the Spanish, for example the land around St. Jago de la Vega (Spanish Town), St. Catherine, St. John and Clarendon and St. Thomas in the Vale, and in the East. Many of the plantation owners had military titles. In Sir Thomas Lynch's papers (he was Governor of Jamaica 1671-74 and 1682-84) he mentions as principal plantations of original owners those of Port Morant (Col. Stokes), Morant (Lord Willoughby), Yallahs (Col. Doyley), Liguanea (Col. Barry), Los Angeles (Col. Ward) and Guanaboa (Col. Barrington). In Edward Doyley's papers (he was Commander in Chief and the first Governor 1655-1662) in the British Library there is a list of people to whom licenses were granted to settle and to some granted army commissions (Add MS 12423 ff. 112-123 reversed). The *Caribbeana* list of wills proved in the PCC (See Wills) also has some of the names of very early settlers (1655-1661).

In 1664, the island was reinforced with 1,000 Barbadians who came to Jamaica with Sir Thomas Modyford, a Barbadian planter. Thus some of the early English settlers of Jamaica went first from England to Barbados and then to Jamaica.

There were also 1,600 English settlers who came to Jamaica from the island of Nevis (near St. Christopher, St. Kitts), but in the time of D'Oyley (ca. 1662) only 400 were still alive, after he took over from General Brayne as commander of the island, and of the 1,200 brought by General Brayne "not fewer hundred left" (quoted from Povey Papers, British Library, Egerton MS 2395).

D'Oyley sent for 250 of the settlers of the Somer Islands (Bermuda) which were so crowded that many of their people removed to Jamaica. I have not yet found lists for any of the Barbadian, Nevis or General Brayne settlers, but some of them may be included in the D'Oyley papers listed above. (Some information on the life and times of D'Oyley, derived from his own notes, may be seen in the article "Edward D'Oyley, 1617-1675" by David Buisseret, *Jamaica Journal*, Vol. 5, No. 1, pp. 6-10, 1971.)

In 1675 many English and their slaves went to Jamaica from Surinam, a total of three ships and 1,231 people. Their names are given in the PRO (TNA, Kew) America and West Indian Calendar for 1675-6, Addenda 1574-1674. Most of these settlers started their lands in St. Elizabeth, and there is a section of the parish known as Surinam.

It is known that a few of the English regicides (persons who were involved with the beheading of Charles I) were given land in Jamaica by Cromwell. Some of them took up this settlement upon the restoration of Charles II. One such family was the Blagrove family which settled in Hanover and St. Ann.

Indentured Servants

When the British conquered Jamaica, there already existed African slaves who had been imported by the Spanish (See Maroons), but the English settlers who patented large areas of land first imported English men and women on indentures of four to seven years to work on their plantations as they did in Barbados, St. Kitts and America. These subjects were sometimes treated very harshly and the climate did not enhance their chances of living. Hence we have very few records of their existence in Jamaica, their deaths coming before the establishment of parish records. A few did serve out their indentures and were absorbed into the indistinguishable English pool of new settlers. Several sources of lists of indentured servants exist in English archives. They do include the larger portion of indentured servants who left England for America, so there may be a great deal to wade through to find West Indian and particularly Jamaican indentured servants. Some of these lists include: *Plantation Indentures (Servants) "Servants to Foreign Plantations, 1654-1671 or 1679"*, 2 vols., Bristol Record Office, 04220/1-2. Volume 2 lists the date 1671 on the cover but actually goes to 1679. The enrollment of these indentures includes servant's name, place of origin (first part of Volume 1), master's name, destination, term of years and conditions of service. These records have been published in London (no date) as *Bristol and America: A record of the first Settlers in the Colonies of North America 1654-1685* compiled and edited by N. Dermott Harding. They have been updated by Peter Wilson Coldham in *The Bristol Registers of Servants sent to Foreign Plantations 1654-1686* (Baltimore: Genealogical Publishing Co., 1988, 491 pp., ISBN 0-8063-1223-8). The largest number of servants from Bristol left in 1685 to Jamaica, but many left before that for Barbados and could have later come to Jamaica.

London servants are enrolled in *Plantation Indentures (Servants) Jan 21, 1682/3 to September 4, 1684. 742 Items*, Greater London Record Office (Middlesex records) MCRO Pl 1-742. These records were on printed forms with the pertinent information filled in, which included the name, address, age and occupation of the servant, the signature or mark of the same, the name, address and occupation of the person to whom he was bound (frequently the ship's master), the place and number of years for which he was bound and the name of the ship and ship's master on which he (or she) would sail. Magistrates and witnesses signed the indentures. Of the 742 remaining existing items, 80 are indentures for Jamaica. Only 21 of these are signed by the servants, the others carrying a mark. Most were indentured for four years. Of the 80, 33 had occupations listed, viz. as accountant, baker, barber, blacksmith, brickmaker, butcher, cooper, cordwainer, gardener, glazier, groom or ostler, miller, sawyer and shoemaker. Of the 33, 14 were husbandman, labourers or ploughmen. An additional three indentures originally from this series are in the collection of the National Library of Jamaica. The names of the indentees were Barenthia England, John Floyd and William Bird of London and the dates the indentures were made is 1683. The *Genealogists Magazine*, the magazine of the Society of Genealogists

London, has abstracts of these indentures prepared by C. D. P. Nicholson under the title "Some Early Emigrants to America" in Vol. 12, No. 1, 1955 through Vol. 13, No. 8, 1960.

The largest collection of indentures of servants for Jamaica is found in the Corporation of London Record Office (Guildhall Library). The earliest are for 1682-1692 and are in a series of 21 large folio volumes known as "The Lord Mayor's Waiting Books". Of these 960 entries in the Lord Mayor's Court, 321 pertain to Jamaica. The entries have been extracted and published as *A List of Emigrants from England to America, 1682-1692* by Michael Ghirelli (Baltimore: Magna Charta Book Co., 1968, 106 pp.). A larger series from 3,117 printed forms of indentures in the Corporation of London Record Office includes 1,219 indentures for Jamaica. The period 1718-1739 is covered, with a few for 1749-1759. These have been compiled by Jack and Marion Kaminkow (Baltimore: Magna Charta Book Co., 1964, 288 pp.) as *A List of Emigrants from England to America 1718-1759*.

Indentured servants leaving from Liverpool have been compiled by Elizabeth French, *A List of Emigrants to America from Liverpool 1697-1707* (1983, Baltimore: Genealogical Publishing Co., 55 pp.)

A site called English America compiled by Thomas Langford http://www.english-america.com/places/jamaica.html#top   has listed people from 1679 to 1773 who sailed to Jamaica . Actually there are very few after 1686. The lists give the ships and passenger names and sometimes the notation of servant to such and such a person.

The PRO (TNA, Kew) does not hold records of indentured servants.

By 1775, very few English immigrants to Jamaica came as indentured servants, because the numbers of slaves were greatly increased. Thus of a series of 9,000+ persons leaving England and Scotland in 1773-1775 only eight of 495 persons going to the West Indies were indentured, whereas more than 4,400 were indentured to persons in North America. (See *Voyagers to the West* by Bernard Bailyn, New York: A. A. Knopf, 1986, 668 pp., ISBN 0-394-51569-2. This is a statistical treatment and does not list names of persons, but fills in a great deal of history, particularly the reasons of immigration to America at that time.) There are however a very few accounts (as late as 1822) of particular artisans and craftsmen apprentices indenturing themselves to Jamaican estate owners, and some of their letters home are found in the manuscript sources in Ingram's *Sources of Jamaican History, 1655-1838*.

Convicts or Persons in Bondage

Jamaica was not a penal colony, but between 1655 and the early 1700s, some persons were transported for crimes (some of which we would now consider trivial) to Jamaica or Barbados. The idea was twofold: to increase the number of settlers and to rid England of its less desirable citizens who would otherwise be imprisoned. Consent to transportation was often given as an alternative choice to imprisonment in England. Like indentured servants, such persons were bound to masters in the colonies, but unlike indentured servants the time of servitude was 7-10 years rather than 4 years. Since some early settlers to Jamaica came from Barbados it is also worth checking for this reason; however, do not expect success, but be delighted if you do find some ancestor.

The book to check is *The Complete book of Emigrants in Bondage, 1614-1775* by Peter Wilson Coldham (1988, Baltimore: Genealogical Publishing Co., 920 pp., ISBN 0-8063-121-1). These records are compiled from court and other legal records in England. By identifying the source, you may be able to search these original English records for additional details on the person's origins, including the trial proceedings. In *The Complete book of Emigrants in Bondage, 1614-1775*, page 917 lists only three ships which had as their destination Jamaica, viz. the *Lewis*, December 1716 (TNA/PRO Treasury T53/25/224), the *Queen Elizabeth*, January 1717 (TNA/PRO Treasury T53/25/225), and the *Christabella*, February 1722.

Persons of Quality and later English Immigrants

The early settlers who eventually ended up building large estates in the early eighteenth century in Jamaica were not necessarily from established landed families in England. However, it is wise to review Hotten's Lists of Persons of Quality. The full citations are: *John Camden Hotten, The original Lists of Persons of Quality... and others Who Went from Great Britain to the American Plantations 1600-1700* (Baltimore: Genealogical Publishing Co., 1980) and *Hotten's List Supplement* (Baltimore: Genealogical Publishing Co., 1983).

For more ordinary folk from the period 1607-1776, Peter W. Coldham has published *The Complete Book of Emigrants*, 4 Volumes, 1607-1776 (Baltimore: Genealogical Publishing Co., 1987-1993). Besides being available in book form, the complete set of four volumes is available on CD-ROM from the Genealogical Publishing Company in which a search feature is included. These lists include the records of T47/9-11, 1773-1775 used by Bernard Bailyn mentioned above.

Less data are currently available to the researcher after the American Revolution (1776) and until emigration records from England began to be kept in 1890. During this period there was a significant rise in people from England hoping to make their fortunes in Jamaica in sugar. The earlier residents had established their estates and often returned to England to build large estates there and become absentee landlords in Jamaica, fanning the lure in spite of the difficulties of climate and financial risk. Their success, it was hoped, could be repeated and many younger sons and black sheep were sent out to learn the sugar planting trade. While some did make it, in comparison to the numbers who tried, there were few, often because they were tied up in debt to mercantile interests in England who supplied the would-be sugar barons with goods and merchandise on the promise of sugar and rum to be produced. Often crops failed, hurricanes or other disasters hit, or costs of slaves were prohibitive to work the new estates or they were poor or indolent managers. It was difficult to extricate the owners from debt and many lawsuits took years to settle.

From the earliest patents of the eighteenth century for land in Jamaica, new patentees had to promise to employ a certain number of white persons in proportion to their slaves. (In fact, all free persons of colour who owned slaves also fell under this so-called deficiency law, and were supposed to hire whites in proportion to their slaves, until this law was repealed in 1813 for this group, but not for white owners.) Whites were usually employed as book keepers, but they hoped to rise through the pyramid of plantation autocracy to overseer, attorney and then owner of some land, then retire to Britain. While death from disease carried off many new arrivals and some in the pyramid, it was not easy to make this transition. A book about some of these adventurers is *Gentlemen of Fortune: the men who made their fortunes in Britain's Slave colonies*, by D. Knight (Frederick Mullen, 1978, 135 pp.).

Another group that was perhaps more successful was the younger sons who were sent out as merchants. After the act of 1807 passed which forbade the importation of slaves into the island, sugar production started to decline, and after the abolition of slavery in 1834, many of the plantations established in the late 1700s became ruinate. Still, many hopefuls came to the plantations in hopes of building a fortune even beginning as book keepers. These immigrants are quite difficult to trace, but some of the lists of persons in that section of this book may be helpful. Church records and deeds do give some data but do not often mention the place of origin in England of such people. Thus if family tradition or oral history is not available, the researcher has a difficult task of extending the immigrant ancestor's line back to England.

The rise of banana plantations did not occasion the influx of British fortune seekers that the sugar plantations did, but some did come out to work in this field. By the 1890s, British immigrants were mainly colonial civil servants, clergymen, schoolteachers, merchants, policemen and military personnel who rotated to the island. Many did not intend to stay permanently, but to retire to England once their service was completed. Some however married into island families and remained. The PRO (TNA, Kew) holds records from 1890-1960 in Board of Trade passenger lists (BT27) of people leaving England for places outside Europe. They need to be searched by date, port of departure and by ship and include names, age, occupation and usually the place of residence in England. I have found a relative leaving in 1890 but it was quite a difficult search.

A recent book chapter examines the White population in Jamaica in the late 1800's. It is: *The White Minority in the Caribbean. Edited by Howard Johnson & Karl Watson Chapter 6. The White Minority in Jamaica at the end of the Nineteenth Century by Patrick Bryan.* (1998 pp. 116-132. Ian Randle, Kingston, Jamaica Publishers. Jamaica ISBN: 976-8123-10-9. James Curry, United Kingdom ISBN:0-85255-746-9. Markus Wiener, Princeton, NJ ISBN: 1-55876-161-6.As you can see this book covers the entire Caribbean and not just Jamaica. In fact the chapters covering other islands are often more comprehensive than the chapter covering Jamaica. However since it treats a subject from a different perspective from about 1850 to the early 1900's it is a useful. Several prominent families particularly merchants of the time are mentioned. The Jews and the Scots are picked out for some discussion of the diversity among the white families. The chapter treats some of the institutions originating in this era by whites. The relationship between the ex-patriate and local whites is explored. The bibliography of the chapter shows that several Daily Gleaner (Newspaper) excerpts are used. *See also Military Records.*

The Daily Gleaner on-line has a series called Pieces in the Past. Included are a section called Out of Many Cultures, The People who came. In this section are The English at: http://www.jamaica-gleaner.com/pages/history/story0063.html

Scots

The Scots had similar experiences in emigrating to Jamaica as the English, but what I treat here are additional references pertaining especially to them. Since James I of England was James VI of Scotland, the records in England after 1655 (the date of British conquest of Jamaica), are often but not always similar. So if your ancestors were Scottish, you should also read the section on England.

Darien – the early Scots Settlers

In the late seventeenth century, a company of Scotland (The Company of Scotland trading to Africa and the Indies) tried to establish a colony in Darien on the Isthmus of Panama. This was protested by Spain and the native Indians were not friendly. Two expeditions were organized; both ended in disaster. The king of England did not approve of the company. An account of these excursions is related in the book *The Darien Disaster: a Scots Colony in the New World 1698-1700* by John Prebble (New York: Holt, Rinehart and Winston, 1968, 366 pp.). The weakened colonists, who called their colony Caledonia or New Caledonia, eventually left their disastrous colony and some of the survivors deserted the ships sailing back to Scotland via New York in Jamaica. When the ships reached Jamaica, there was little relief (prohibited by the king) for the 300 or less survivors, and thus to sustain themselves in food and clothing, many sold themselves as servants to the plantations both in 1698 and in 1700. Many settled in St. Elizabeth, which was not yet divided into St. Elizabeth and Westmoreland (which occurred in 1703). While there are many persons' names in the index of the book *The Darien Disaster*, there is no indication of which men and women settled in Jamaica. A list of the 1698 group that died in Caledonia is given in the bibliography.

An excerpt from *Singer's Quarterly* which came into my hands, has the following to say about the Scots in Jamaica:

> Visitors to the Parish of Westmoreland will find the names of places nearly all contiguous to each other, where these refugees were settled, Blauwearie, Bognie, Cairn Curran, Caledonia, Carawina, Culloden, Galloway, Glasgow, Glencoe, Glenislay, Lennox, Strathbogie, Whitehouse, Whithorn are some of the most important.

The next major invasion of Jamaica took place after the last attempt of the Jacobites to restore the Stuart dynasty to the throne was definitely crushed at Culloden by the British troops under the command of the German Duke of Cumberland. So ruthlessly did he deal with conquered patriots that he earned the sobriquet of The Butcher. The colonies seemed their only place of refuge and many of them came to Jamaica. The Mackintosh family, who were known to have sheltered Bonnie Prince Charlie and so could not hope to be included in the Act of Indemnity, were among the first to arrive. Their home in Scotland was called Moy and when they settled here on the uplands of St. Thomas, they named their place Moy Hall. Their monuments may still be seen there.

One of those refugees, a Mackenzie, must have been a bit of a wag. He chose as his new settlement's site near to the very centre of the Island, remarking that he thought it was far enough from the tender mercies of the ruthless German Duke. That place still goes by the name of Farenough.

The Murrays were also deeply involved in the Forty-five, and although one of them, Murray of Broughton, afterwards turned traitor, some of the Clan found conditions at home too hot for their comfort. In more that one locality in Jamaica there is a place called Broughton.

The abolition of slavery in the British possessions was decreed in 1834, and the slaves were placed on an apprenticeship system, the complete enfranchment taking place in 1838. There was great anxiety amongst the planters as to whether the emancipated workers would continue to serve for wages on the estates; so they decided to make sure by supplying the labour from abroad. Hundreds of thousands of pounds were spent by the Legislature in financing this immigration, and again the eyes of all concerned were turned to Scotland. In 1837 a shipment of Scots arrived and were [sic] settled in the cooler hinterland in the parish of Portland. They called their settlement Altamont, where their descendants are still to be seen, few however are of unmixed blood.

In January 1841, another shipment arrived consisting of 322 from Stranrear, and towards the end of that year the population was increased by 600 who sailed from Aberdeen and London. The majority of these were Scots. Some were settled in the highlands of St. Elizabeth, some went to St. Ann, near to Guy's Hill; where there is still to be seen a colony of their descendants at Middlesex.

Brayne was the first of a number of Scottish Governors of Jamaica. Two of them as we have seen were the Earls of Balcarres and Elgin. They were the only two who left their names at places in the Island.

It is therefore not to be wondered at that in the middle of the eighteenth century it was ascertained that about one third of those colonists of European birth were natives of Scotland, and to remove the possibility of their being regarded as descendants of the rogues and vagabonds of Cromwell's time. Long the historian goes on to say that one hundred of the name of Campbell were counted all claiming alliance with the Argyll family.

The following is a List of Scottish names not given already. Annandale in the parish of St. Ann still owned by a Scot. Argyll in Hanover originally established by a member of the Clan Campbell. Arthur's Seat in Clarendon. Anyone who has seen the original frowning over the city of Edinburgh will at once recognise the resemblance. There is another place with this name in Trelawny. Birnanwood. Some reader of Shakespeare must have named this place in Portland. If a tunnel were made under the Blue Mountains to the southern slope of St. Andrew it would come out at Dunsinane. Auchendoun and Auld Aur are names in Westmoreland associated with the Darien settlers. Auchendolly is in the parish of St. James and Auchtembeddie is in Manchester where we shall also find Dalkeith, Dunrobin, Knockpatrick, Melrose, and Struan (the present Laird of Struan is a Jamaican), Ben Lomand, Dundee, Dunedin, Gilneck, Kilnarneck, are to be found in the parish of St. Elizabeth, so is Denkeld.

To St. Ann we go to find Berriedale (there is another in Portland), Dornock, Dumbarton, Edinburgh, Huntly, Inverness, Leith and Turnberry. In St. Catherine we have Carew Castle and Tullock. In St. Andrew we shall find Clydesdale and Kintrye. Hanover testifies to the presence of the Scot at Damally, Haddo. Knockalva — the well known house of the Malcolms of Poltolloch. In St. James there is Deeside, Kilpatrick and Wemyss. Trelawny has Greenock, Roslyn, Tweedsdale and Ythanside. In Clarendon there is another Inverness and Monymusk the home of the Grants. Descendants of the Clan still live at the original Scottish home and the property in Jamaica was originally settled by one of them. In St. Mary there is Kinfauns.

All these testify to the presence and activities of the Scot in every nook and cranny of the Island.

The reference to the Jacobites can be expanded upon in the book *The Original Scots colonists of Early America, 1612-1783* by David Dobson (Baltimore, Maryland: Genealogical Publishing Co. Inc., 1989, ISBN 0-8063-129-39-4). This listing of people who went to America and the West Indies has been compiled from many sources. The list of 7,180 people includes many of the Jacobites who settled in the West Indies, particularly Barbados and Jamaica in 1716/7 and 1747. The largest contingent appeared to have traveled on the ship *St. George* or *Carteret* and arrived in Jamaica in 1747, but there were quite a number in 1716/7 as well. This book however includes many other Scots who immigrated to Jamaica, before and after the Jacobite uprisings. Occasionally Darien survivors are mentioned. However, since the book ends in 1783, it does not include the immigrants, noted in the *Singer's Quarterly* piece, who immigrated in 1837 and 1841. I might add that contrary to the *Singer's* writer's implication, the Scots were not the only labourers who were recruited from Europe after the end of slavery. The English, Irish and Germans were also recruited to Jamaica with promises of land. Miss Inez Sibley in her book on Jamaican place names ascribes the origin of Farenough to a Darien George McKenzie, not a Jacobite. Miss Sibley's book, as mentioned before, has quite a bit of genealogy as she describes the origin of the names of places.

Sugar Factors

As with the immigrants from England for the period from 1775-1783 to 1890, it is difficult to track the Scottish immigrants to Jamaica. Yet this was the time when the number of sugar estates was rapidly increasing, and many were lured to the Sugar Islands to seek their fortune. An analysis of some of these sugar factors and comparison to Maryland's tobacco factors is contained in the book: *Sojourners in the Sun: Scottish Migrants in Jamaica and the Chesapeake, 1740-1800* by Alan L. Karras (Ithaca, NY: Cornell University Press, 1992, 231 pp., ISBN 0-8014-2691-X). They are called sojourners because they did not intend to remain in Jamaica or settle permanently, but rather to make their fortunes and return home to live a grand life. While some progressed to landownership, many did not realize their dream of returning to Scotland. The author suggests that the cost of living in

Scotland and the debts for goods and slaves which were not realized, played a part in this reason for remaining in the island. In other words, they could not realize enough from selling their property in Jamaica to live in the expected manner in Scotland.

Missionaries and Clergy

The Presbyterians and Methodists were among the early non-conformists to come to Jamaica to minister to the slaves. Among the missionaries, several were Scots. Records of clergy sent to Jamaica are possibly found among the respective church documents in England and Scotland. (See under Church Vital Records.)

In the 1844 census, 1,523 persons born in Scotland were counted. *See also under Military records.*

Welsh

The cadence of Jamaican speech has often been remarked to resemble the Welsh cadence. However, there is not a great deal of evidence that the Welsh were a large proportion of the United Kingdom immigrants who came to Jamaica, thus imparting their speech patterns to the inhabitants. There are several place names that obviously come from Wales. These include Llandewey (St. Thomas), Penrhyne (Clarendon), Llandilo, Anglesey (Westmoreland), Llandovery, Milford Haven (St. Ann), Llandraff Pen, Pantrepant (Trelawny), Pembroke Hall, Llanrumney, Pencarne (St. Mary: the latter two were once owned by Sir Henry Morgan, originally Welsh), Phantillanda and Phantillands (St. Elizabeth). Miss Inez Sibley claims Ythanside as a Welsh place name, not Scottish as claimed by the *Singer's Quarterly* article mentioned in the Scots section.

The Bristol Registers of Servants sent to Foreign Plantations, 1654-1686, and the *List of Emigrants to America from Liverpool* (see English section for complete citations) do include some people who were drawn from Wales, Bristol being the closest large port to Wales. Other than that I have not been able to find any records which separately describe Welsh immigrants to Jamaica, and all other English sources should be searched. Sir Henry Morgan, the pirate and buccaneer and later lieutenant-governor, is the most famous Welshman of Jamaica.
See also Military Records.

Irish

Unlike America which was the destination of a large number of Irish settlers after the Potato Famine in the nineteenth century, Jamaica was not a preferred place of refuge. I suppose there were several reasons, such as it being still an English colony, the established religion being Anglican not Roman Catholic, and the decline of the sugar estates after slavery was abolished, signaling that fortunes were not easily made. Still there were a number who did reach the island. Hamilton Brown, the founder of Brown's Town, St. Ann, was an Irishman from Antrim. John Sullivan became Provost Marshall of Jamaica and was from an Irish family. The place names mentioned by Inez Sibley are not as numerous for Ireland as they are for Scotland or even Wales, and most seem to signal Northern Ireland as the place of origin, e.g. Armagh. Irish Town in St. Andrew was a place of settlement of some Irish.

A great deal of speculation on internet newsgroups pertains to the so-called Black Irish or Irish Slaves, who various authors maintain were sent to the West Indies by Oliver Cromwell and were treated as slaves. Supposedly 50,000 boys, women and girls were sent. I can find no evidence of this. One history book reports that Cromwell proposed to send 1,000 Irish women to Jamaica to populate it. But no one seems to have verified that he actually did so. Irish names are not that common in the early vital records. The white population in 1662 (after Cromwell lost power) was less than 5,000 with a 2:1 ratio of men to women. So it seems hardly likely that the 50,000 figure could pertain to Jamaica, although some could have been sent to the other islands. In the index to the RCS there is listed a book which is entitled *Whence the Black Irish of Jamaica?* by J. J. Williams (New York: MacVeagh, 1932, 97 pp.).This book leaves open the possibility that some of the Irish sent to Barbados later came to Jamaica, but it too says that evidence of Cromwellian contingents do not seem to have been verified. See later in this section where Irish indentured people were recruited against the advice of many in Ireland who felt they would be treated as slaves. This may be where some of the misunderstanding arises. For an opposite point of view see Rob Mullally's site http://www.thewildgeese.com/pages/jamone.html. He believes that many more Irish came to Jamaica through Barbados than population statistics of Jamaica bear out. At his site he lists Tom Redcam as an Irishman, but as a relative of mine, I know he was not. His father was married in the Anglican church in Vere.

Besides the individual person mentioned in history books, the first reference to Irish settlers I have found is the justification used by the Roman Catholic Church to re-establish a church in the early 1800s to meet the needs of their French, Haitian and Irish congregations in Jamaica (See Church Records under Roman Catholic). However, Irishmen could have come with the invading army and in contingents of servants leaving from British ports before this time (See under England). Ships which regularly left Bristol in the late eighteenth century and early nineteenth century called at Cork before sailing for the West Indies and could have taken a small number of Irish passengers.

After emancipation the planters, among them Hamilton Brown, attempted to recruit Irish settlers for replacing the estate slaves. By December 1840 this stirred up a lot of displeasure in Ireland, particularly at Limerick, and anti-slavery abolitionists attempted to dissuade any potential settlers from participating by labeling the recruiters as agents for Irish Slaves. This is chronicled in an article in the *Jamaica Journal* by Carl H. Senior entitled *"Robert Kerr: Emigrants of 1840 Irish Slaves for Jamaica" (Jamaica Journal*, No. 42, pp. 104-116, 1978). The *Robert Kerr* was the ship. In the article is mentioned that 121 Irishmen had left on the ship *James Ray*, a brig owned by Hamilton Brown of Jamaica, from Belfast in December 1835. These families came from Ballymoney, County Antrim and they settled in St. Ann, the parish of Hamilton Brown. In 1836, Hamilton Brown imported at least 185 Irishmen for St. Ann. In January 1840, 136 Irish were transported in the *New Phoenix*, from County Kildare to estates in Clarendon, and to Boroughbridge and Rosetta in St. Ann. This early recruitment passed without comment, but the recruitment in December 1840, it was feared, was a massive plan to import 50,000 Irishmen to Jamaica, where they would be treated like slaves. After a great hue and cry, 127 immigrants left on January 11, 1841, on the *Robert Kerr*, with a missionary (the Rev. Oliver Frost) to administer to their spiritual needs. They were not however the very best class of people for whom the recruiters had hoped (class 1 labourers and artisans). This immigration turned out badly; about 25 died of yellow fever, typhus, etc., in the first year. Others deserted their places where indentured and congregated in Kingston grog shops, where drinking rum became the occupation.

Importation of Irish settlers to the highlands of Jamaica ceased in September 1841, and between 1842 and 1845 only 42 immigrants, Scots and British immigrated to the island. This ended the Jamaican Legislature's drive to recruit Europeans to the island to occupy upland lands so that the emancipated slaves could not find land to settle. They next concentrated their efforts on Africans, and Asians. References in this article contain some names of Irish immigrants. The term "Irish Slaves" apparently stuck even 150 years later with speculations that this was a regular occurrence since the time of Cromwell. There is little evidence in Jamaica that large numbers of indentured people came prior to the waves of 100-150/ship in 1835-1842. In the 1844 census, 1,298 persons born in Ireland were counted.

From the Daily Gleaner on line is the piece Out of Many Cultures, The People who Came: The Irish
http://www.jamaica-gleaner.com/pages/history/story0058.htm

German

As mentioned, the Scots and the Irish were not the only people recruited to fill the vacant spots in the estates after emancipation. The Germans were recruited not only for this purpose but to eventually live in the highlands of Jamaica after they had served their time and thus occupy land which was then not readily available to the ex-slaves. An account of this immigration has been written by Francis J. Osborne, S.J. "German Immigration to Jamaica" (*Historical Society Bulletin*, Vol. 6, No. 2, pp. 12-19). It was based on a paper read at the Fourth Conference of Caribbean Historians (University of the West Indies, Mona, April 9-14, 1972), by Professor Douglas Hall entitled, "Bountied European Immigration into Jamaica, with special reference to the German settlement at Seaford Town up to 1850" (see below for published version of this talk). The reason that this interested Father Osborne was that two-thirds of the German immigrants at Seaford Town were Roman Catholics.

The first immigration was advanced with the approval of the Jamaican government by a Mr. Solomon Myers, a German settler who had acquired a property above Buff Bay in the parish of St. George. In 1833 he went to Germany to recruit labourers. He returned in May 1834 from the town of Bremen with 65 people including 25 men, 18 women, 21 children and 2 infants born on the 106-day voyage. They were mainly tradesmen, spinners, knitters, tailors, coppersmiths, one gunsmith, weavers, ploughmen and axemen, and were settled by Myers on a part of the estate which Myers called New Brunswick after the district from which they came. But the scheme was not a success and many of the workers left the plantation for Kingston and other parts of the island. This did not deter Myers, and another 506 persons whom his brother in Germany recruited arrived on December 25, 1834, on the ship *Olberes* from Bremen. Of the 506 immigrants, 150 Germans went to the estate of

Mr. Robert Watt of Montego Bay; and Mr. Hamilton Brown of Brown's Town, St. Ann, took 150. Mr. James Hilton accepted 45 Germans whom he placed on his estate Alva in the Dry Harbour Mountains. Dr. Spaulding with some others claimed 120 immigrants and Mr. Samuel Anderson of Montego Bay another 20 people, leaving 21 for Myers.

Another importer was William Lemonious, a German-born immigrant who brought 800 Germans to the island between 1835 and 1837, the largest number of which, 249, were settled at Seaford Town in Westmoreland. Most of these were from Westphalia, only 28 being from Waldeck. They were bound for five years, after which they would have a few acres of land, 1/2 acre for the head of the family and 1/4 acre for each additional member. Some of these immigrants planted ginger, from which they made such a good income that they were able to buy passages to the United States and settle down in the Midwest. Several of the Seaford Town settlers are named in the above piece. After 1837, support for food rations was cut and the immigrants had to make it on their own. Father Osborne also related early conditions in the settlement and how the Roman Catholic church met the spiritual needs of the Seaford Town Germans. Another perspective on the Seaford Town Germans is given in "Bountied European immigration into Jamaica with special reference to the German settlement at Seaford Town up to 1850" by Douglas Hall (*Jamaica Journal*, Part 1, Vol. 8, No. 4, pp. 48-54, 1974, and Part 2, Vol. 9, No. 1, pp. 2-9, 1974/5). Present-day descendants of these Germans are still to be found in the island as they intermarried with Jamaicans. In the Anglican Church records of St. Ann, many of these German settlers are recorded where they are termed Small Settlers. The names include Helwig, Hahn, Haultaufdeheid and Lannaman as well as others. In the census of 1844, 615 persons born in Germany were counted.

A thoroughly researched historical study is "German immigrants in Jamaica 1834-8" by Carl H. Senior (*Journal of Caribbean History*, Vols. 10 & 11, 1978, pp. 25-53).

The Daily Gleaner on line has a piece Out of Many People, The People who came: The Germans at:
http://www.jamaica-gleaner.com/pages/history/story0060.htm

Jews

There were Jews in Jamaica during the Spanish occupation (one named Don Acosta signed the surrender to General Venables), but I do not know how many remained after the British conquered the island.

Some certainly did as evidenced in the old cemetery at Hunts Bay. However, the acceptance of Oliver Cromwell of Jews in England and the lifting of the ban on their residing there also applied to Jamaica, and several Jewish families moved to Jamaica. Most of the Jews who settled in Jamaica up to the 1770s were Sephardim, originally from Spain and Portugal via Holland or England. It has been estimated that 10 percent of the Spanish and Portuguese congregation in London (Bevis Marks) had ties to Jamaica. There is evidence that there were 800 Jews in Jamaica by 1735. A short article on the Jews in Jamaica is found in the RCS library entitled "Documents relating to the history of the Jews in Jamaica and Barbados in the time of William III" by F. Cundall, D. Davis, and A. M. Friedenberg (5 pp., 1915). Early Jews in Jamaica were merchants, and held land, but they had to pay heavy taxes up to 1741 and could not vote until 1826; they began to hold judicial and other offices in the 1840s.

Some of the articles and books about Jamaican Jewry include: "Spanish & Portuguese Jews of Jamaica: mid 16th–mid 17th c" by Rosemarie DePass Scott (*Jamaica Journal*, No. 43, pp. 90-100, March 1979). This article includes an example of a headstone from the Hunt's Bay Cemetery. Names mentioned in this article are De Mesquita, Torris, Jacobson, Rodriques, Jacob, Gibay, Mendez Guterez, Levy, Soares, Gomez, most of whom were merchants. Daniel Israel Lopez Laguna was a poet of Spanish Town in 1674. Jews were also physicians, and those mentioned as practicing in Kingston in the early 1700s were DeLeon, Garcia, Henriques and Jacob Adolphus.

Other articles are "The New World sets an example for the Old: the Jews of Jamaica and Political Rights, 1661-1831" by S. J. Hurwitz and E. F. Hurwitz (*American Jewish Historical Quarterly*, Vol. 55, No. 1, pp. 37-56, Sept. 1965), and "The Jews of Jamaica: a historical view" by Benjamin Schlesinger (*Caribbean Quarterly*, Vol. 13, No. 1, pp. 46-53, March 1967). The Hurwitzes have written other articles published in the *American Jewish Historical Society* entitled "A Beacon for Judaism: The first Fruits of the West" (1966), and "Jamaica: a Historical Portrait" (New York: Praeger, 1971). In 1964 J. P. Rosenbloom had "Notes on the Jews: Tribute in Jamaica" published in London (Jewish Historical Society of England).

Short pieces written by Jamaican Jews include "The Jews' Tribute to Jamaica" by George Fortunatus Judah (New York: American Historical Society, 1909), and by the same author "History of Jews in Jamaica: Evidence of Forgotten Records" (*Daily Telegraph*, 1900-1901). *A Panorama of Jamaican Jewry: the tercentenary of the official founding of the Jewish Community of Jamaica, BWI, 5415-5725, 1655-1955* was written by Harry Phillips Silverman (Rabbi) (Kingston, Gleaner Co., 1955, 19 pp., map).

The most comprehensive inclusion of names is found in *A Record of the Jews in Jamaica from the English Conquest to the present time* by Jacob A. P. M. Andrade [ed. by Basil Parke] (Kingston, Jamaica: Jamaica Times, 1941, 282 pp., 2 maps). Besides the extensive listings of prominent men and women, this book includes descriptions of synagogues and their paraphernalia, extracts of wills donating legacies to the synagogues and charitable institutions of the congregations, and epitaphs and memorials in many of the places of burial of the Jews in Jamaica. This book can be found in many research university libraries in the U.S.; unfortunately it does not have a good index. There are also a number of names mentioned in "A survey of the History of Jamaica Jewry in early times", written in the *Daily Gleaner Newspaper* (November 26, 1937, pp. 13, 23). This article was written at a time of great anti-Semitism in Jamaica as elsewhere in the world and the writer tries to demonstrate to the audience the contributions which individual Jews had made to the island.

The Daily Gleaner Newspaper started as the *DeCordeva Advertizing Sheet and Daily Gleaner* in 1834 and was owned by a Jewish family. Births, deaths and marriages in the vital records of this newspaper were very heavily Kingston Jews, up to the early 1900s. They preferred this medium to the *Royal Gazette*. However this was not cheap; in 1904, it cost 3 shillings per entry, or 7/6d for 3 days' notice. (See Newspapers.) There is also a book by B. W. Korn on *The Haham DeCordeva of Jamaica* (Philadelphia: M. Jacob Inc., 1966).

Three more recent books are *The Portuguese Jews of Jamaica by Mordechai Arbell*. (Jamaica:Canoe Press, 2000, 70pp. ISBN 976-8125-69-1).This slim little volume takes us from the Portuguese Jews who settled Jamaica during the time of the Spanish occupation to early in the 20th century. It is richly developed with black and white illustrations. The chapters include the Jews of Port Royal, Jewish settlements of Jamaica, Jewish rights and disabilities as well as Jewish economic activities. The last chapter under the heading Cultural life deals briefly with the lives of noteworthy Jews. There is a short list as an illustration of Jews in Jamaica and Barbados in the late 1600's. A list of cemeteries taken from other sources is listed in the appendix. Though it does not add a great deal to the other Jewish sources, it is interesting for its illustrations of the synagogues of Kingston and its bibliography. *The Lindo Legacy by Jackie Ranston*. (London: Toucan Books, 2000. ISBN

1-903435-00-5. 144 p., ill., plates, (some col.), traces the fortunes of a prominent Jamaican Sephardic Jewish family, from the Spanish and Portuguese Inquisitions, through their travels from Amsterdam to London, and then to Jamaica. The book was commissioned by Blanche Lindo Blackwell and is meticulously researched. While not a definitive history of the Sephardic Jews in Jamaica, It is a fascinating study of how one Sephardic family settled there and made its fortune, first in Kingston, then in Falmouth, and eventually in Costa Rica

The third book is by Delevante and Alberga published in 2006. *The Island of one People: An account of the History of the Jews of Jamaica* by Marilyn Delevante and Anthony Alberga Kingston and Miami:Ian Randle Publishers 2006 223pp   ISBN 976-637-212-8. Delevante and Alberga have carried forward the descriptions of Andrade into the beginning of the 21st Century of the Jews in Jamaica. Thus descriptions of the synagogues, cemeteries and their present conditions are included. Biographies of Jewish personalities and Merchants are detailed and specific treatment is given to eight families in separate chapters namely the Lindo, deLisser, Myers, deCordover, Ashenheim, Henriques, Matalon and Alberga familes. The book is beautifully illustrated with pictures or photographs on practically every page, well annotated and indexed..

Synagogues: For a full description of synagogues, read Andrade and Delevante (above). The first synagogue in Jamaica appears to have been in Port Royal or Spanish Town, however it soon was augmented by synagogues in Kingston. Altogether Andrade lists a total of nine synagogues existing in the island at one time or another. The 1878 Directory of Kingston gives the following entry:

> English and German Synagogue, Kaal Kadosh Shahar Yoshare,
> Founded 1737: Rebuilt 1839, Treasurer George Levy.

In 1891 in an obituary in the *Gleaner*, a Mrs. Rebecca Nunes Rebeiro left contributions to both synagogues in Kingston: the Spanish and Portuguese Synagogue in East Street (Sephardic), and the English and German Synagogue (Askenazi) in Orange Street.

In the early 1900s the Kingston synagogues combined into the United Synagogue of Israelites and now there is only one building at Duke Street (rebuilt after the 1907 earthquake).

Vital records on microfilm for Jews have already been covered in Vital Records – Non-Conformist Records. And Jewish cemeteries are described in the chapter on Monumental Inscriptions. Wills of Jews in Jamaica start as early as 1673 and some are recorded in the PCC.

A site on Jamaican Jewish families is http://www.sephardim.org/index.html. A collection of links is at: http://www.haruth.com/Jews Jamaica.html

From Pieces in the past in the Daily Gleaner online there is Out of Many Cultures, The People who came: The Jews in Jamaica at http://www.jamaica-gleaner.com/pages/history/story0054.htm

See also Naturalization.

French – Haiti

France was often at war with England in the Caribbean, so not many French people settled in Jamaica until the Black Revolution in Haiti. England had sent troops into Haiti in the late 1790s, but so many of them died of disease they never mixed with the French in Haiti or St. Domingue. After Toussaint L'Overature took over Haiti, many of the French fled to Jamaica. The British government in Jamaica was very concerned that the negro revolution in Haiti would spread to the slaves in Jamaica; they were not particularly welcoming to the French with their slaves who fled from the same revolution. Some of this is reflected in Lady Nugent's Journal (See History). From these refugee families descended several well-known Jamaican families. The best sources on these refugees are some typescript books held by the NLJ written by a Louis Malabre. They are:

• *Baptismal, marriage and burial record of the French families of St. Domingue and Jamaica. together with dossiers and other miscellaneous data {18th to 19th cent?}* by Louis C. Malabre (1 volume binder, Institute of Jamaica [now the National Library of Jamaica], MS 37).

Also:

• *The French Families of Saint Domingue and Jamaica, British West Indies* by Louis C. Malabre (3 volumes, illustrated, Institute of Jamaica, MS 37).

Also:

• *Records of a vanishing age: portraits and souvenirs* by Louis C. Malabre (1 volume binder, Institute of Jamaica, MS 37).

These three are all listed as being in the Institute of Jamaica, MS 37. Louis Malabre donated them to the NLJ in 1949 and 1964. Patricia Jackson has transcribed some of the Malabre documents at http://jamaicanfamilysearch.com/Samples/bmalabre.htm. This site has several free pages, but to obtain the full advantage of the information, membership is required. It is however possible to join for a modest fee, e.g. in 2006, it costs $8.00 for a month. Another author who has written on the topic is Patrick Bryan, who wrote "Émigrés, conflict and reconciliation. The French émigrés in the nineteenth century Jamaica" (*Jamaica Journal*, Vol. 7, No. 3, pp. 13-19, Sept. 1973, with bibliography). Another article is "The French Influence on Jamaica" by H. P. Jacobs (*Jamaica Historical Review*, Vol. 11, pp. 5-49, 1978).

Besides Kingston and Spanish Town, two parishes where some French refugees settled were Portland and St. Ann. One of my ancestors, a Charles Dussard of DonDon, Haiti, was one of the refugees who settled in St. Ann (1803-1835) in the coffee growing area (Dry Harbour Mountains) which was related to the former occupation that he had in Haiti.

The LDS church holds microfilmed church records of Haiti from about 1777 to 1790 in many of the Catholic churches in Haiti (FHL Catalog: Haiti/Church records). If you are lucky to find a vital record in these films it might lead you back to the area in France from which the immigrant came, especially in burials (sepulchre). Many of the leading citizens of Haiti signed as witnesses to marriages and burials, so even if you do not find a vital record you might find a signature of an ancestor. These records are of course in French. There are also deeds recorded by notaries, to which there are some indexes in the FHLibrary. The original deeds are in Aix-en-Provence in France for which you will need to employ a records researcher. It is interesting that these deeds probably resided for quite a while in Spanish Town, when they were brought to Jamaica by refugees. Some of them show insect damage which was probably from their storage in Spanish Town.

There are also in the TNA in London, some admiralty records which might yield some data. They are Adm 103 Medical Departments Registers: Prisoners of War. In particular:

Adm 103/191, 1798-1801 - Jamaica. Dutch and French.
Adm 103/193, 1803 - Jamaica. French.
Adm 103/199, 1806 - Jamaica. French.
Adm 103/200-202, 1806-1809 - Jamaica. French and Spanish.
Adm 103/574-576, 1793-1806 - Jamaica. French.
Adm 103/620, 1803-1812 - Jamaica. Deaths of prisoners. French.
Adm 103/627, 1804-1806 - Jamaica. Deaths of prisoners. French.

There is also a book by A. DeClairanville entitled *Les Francais Prisoniers de Guerre a la Jamaique en 1803 et 1804 ou les Anglais tel qu'il sont*, but I do not have the publication information. This book may be in the Bibliotheque Nationale in Paris.

In the British Library Humanities 2, is found a Bulletin in which an article appears called *Les Colons de Saint-Dominigue passés à la Jamaique 1792-1835* par *Philip Wright et Gabriel Debein*. (Notes d'histoire coloniale No 168. Extrait du Bulletin de la Société d'Historie de la Guadeloupe No 26 4° Trimestre 1975). This has a Table of Names from page 205-217 of people who came from Haiti to Jamaica with page numbers to where some additional data in the article may be found.

A book set in Haiti, which establishes the flavour of Haiti during the turn-of-the-century revolution, 1791-1803, is *The Haitian Journal of Lieutenant Howard, York Hussars, 1796-1798* by Roger Norman Buckley (Knoxville: University of Tennessee Press, 1985, 194 pp., ISBN 0-87049-476-7). The York Hussars were part of the contingent of British soldiers sent to Haiti, and the lieutenant kept a diary of his experiences there.

Two articles which give some information on the French interaction with Jamaica are: "A Frenchman looks at Jamaica in 1706", edited by Dr. David Buisseret (*Jamaica Journal*, Vol. 2, No. 3, pp. 5-8, 1968) and "The French Invasion of Jamaica 1694" by David Buisseret (*Jamaica Journal*, Vol. 16, No. 3, pp. 31-33, 1983). Although neither of these two articles addresses immigrants to Jamaica, they are interesting for the perspective of the French attitude towards Jamaica, and especially the latter gives some flavour of why the British inhabitants of Jamaica were fearful of invasion in the early days of the colony.

The 1844 census counted 1,342 people who were born in Haiti or France. The church records of the Roman Catholic Church are covered under Vital Records – Non-Conformist Records, and contain some information pertinent to French refugees from Haiti.

East Indian

After emancipation and after the failure of various attempts to bring Europeans to Jamaica to work in place of the freed slaves, the Jamaican estate owners turned to Asia. Workers from India were recruited to work in the cane fields. The first indentured Indian workers to arrive in Jamaica in 1845 were 200 males, 20 females and 33 children under age 12 years. By 1848, 5,500 had been recruited and by 1900 an additional 23,395 had come to Jamaica to work. Even in the twentieth century another 7,500 were recruited until the practice was stopped in 1917. The time of indenture was planned to be a minimum of five years and their passages were to be paid for return to India. The latter part was seldom fulfilled. Most of the recruited labourers came from Northern India. A breakdown of the states where some of them were from is given in "Indian heritage in Jamaica" by Lakshmi Mansingh and Ajai Mansingh (*Jamaica Journal*, Vol. 10, Nos. 2-4, pp. 10-19, December 1976). An expansion of this article is: *Home Away From Home: 150 Years of Indian Presence in Jamaica 1845-1995* by Laxmi Mansingh and Ajai Mansingh Kingston; Ian Randle Publishers, 1999, 160pp ISBN 976-8123-38-9. Indians were settled in Jamaica mainly in the parishes of St. Thomas, Portland, St. Mary, Westmoreland and Clarendon. Malaria and hookworm infestation played havoc with their health. Estimates are that of the 5,500 recruited in 1848, 1,503 persons died of these diseases. They were not allowed to leave the estate; leaving was unlawful and resulted in a prison term. Most of the labourers were Hindu, followed by Muslim, a few Christians and other religions. Many left India because of the poor conditions there and the enticements put out by the recruiters, and even after their indentured time was up, did not return. Either they could not afford the return passage, they had established families in Jamaica or they judged that the conditions in India were not improved enough to return. "Transients to Citizens: The development of a Settled East Indian Community" by Verene A. Shepherd (*Jamaica Journal*, Vol. 18, No. 3, pp. 17-26, 1985) tells of the settling in to Jamaica of these immigrants. This article was summarized from a thesis and the final work has now been published as: *Transients to Settlers: The Experience of Indians in Jamaica 1845-1950* by Verene Shepherd (Leeds, England, University of Warwick and Peepal Tree Books, ISBN 0948833 32 7, 1994, 281pp). The eight chapters include an overview, Indians as Indentured settlers, Transients to settlers, Economic Activities and socioeconomic conditions of Indian Settlers, Missionary Activities, Education and perhaps the most interesting Social Customs and Institutions and pressure to Conform. In the latter marriage, divorce and disposal of the dead are treated. An execellent bibliography and index are included with each chapter having notes and references. This bibliography will give you a very detailed idea of where additional sources are available. There are several tables and figures with for example economic data, a map of where in India indentured labourers were recruited, and where immigrants from one ship were sent to Estates in Jamaica.   Other sources of information about the Indian workers are given in *East India (Indentured Labour): report to the Government of*

*India on the conditions of Indian immigrants in four British colonies and
Surinam Part II. Surinam, Jamaica, Fiji and general remarks* by James
McNeill and Chimman Lal (London: HM Stationary Office, 1915, pp.
201-43, Command Papers, Cd 7745), and *East Indian cane workers in
Jamaica* by Allen S. Ehrlich (Ph.D. thesis, 1969, University of Michigan,
available on microfilm from University Microfilms, Ann Arbor,
Michigan).

Some Indians converted to Christianity, and records of baptisms,
and deaths are to be found in Anglican church parishes. Many were
designated with the term "coolie" which originally meant dedicated
labourers, but later developed a rather negative connotation. A Hindu
temple was built in St. Andrew on the Hagley Park Road in the late
1970s, and Muslims had mosques in Spanish Town and Westmoreland.
However since these post-dated Civil Registration, it is unlikely that any
records of vital events would exist that would not be available from the
governments sources. Prior to Civil Registration, many records might not
exist, because it was not customary at weddings for example to record
the event until much Westernization had occurred. In the 1943 census,
21,500 East Indians were recorded, with 5,000 East Indian Coloured,
indicating that there was not a great deal of intermarriage or cohabitation
with other ethnic groups up to the 1940s in Jamaica. Many Indians later
became prominent merchants, particularly of jewelry, in Kingston and
elsewhere.

The TNA/PRO in London has Colonial Office records which pertain
to the immigration of Indian labourers. CO 318 has sections on Indians
who went as labourers in 1843-1873 to the West Indies. Later records are
continued in CO 323 in immigration department records in CO 571 for
1913-1920. In the book *Tracing your West Indian Ancestors, 2nd edition*
by Guy Grannum, there is an illustration of a list of Indian immigrants
from the ship *Newcastle* who were indentured to serve in St. Vincent in
1868. Other English and Indian sources are suggested by Grannum.

There is from Pieces in the Past: in the Daily Gleaner on line
entitled Out of Many Cultures, The people who came: The Indians
http://www.jamaica-gleaner.com/pages/history/story0057.htm

Chinese

The second group of labourers recruited from Asia were the
Chinese. However many did not remain in the cane fields for very long.
They first entered the wholesale grocery trade and later the retail grocery
trade. Many Chinese were the only retail grocers in country villages —

they ran the proverbial "Chinaman shop". Unlike in America, few Chinese tended to laundry retailing. In contrast to the East Indians, they did mix with the other ethnic groups, so that the 1943 census lists 6,900 Chinese and 5,500 Chinese coloured. Later Chinese entered banking and real estate, and many became leading merchants in Kingston. Many at least in Kingston became Roman Catholics. In the 1950s the Catholic boys' and girls' high schools drew many of the Chinese children (both Catholics and non-Catholics) to their institutions. In the 1980s and '90s some of the wealthiest Jamaicans were of Chinese descent.

A book written in both Chinese and English which gives extensive biographical information on Jamaican Chinese is *The Chinese in Jamaica*, edited by Lee Tom Yin (Kingston: Chung San News, 1963, 260 pp.). This book, a copy of which is found in the RCS library, gives the information that the Chinese came in three waves. The first arrivals were in 1854, when 472 Chinese labourers on the railway construction in Panama demanded to leave Panama. They were sent to Jamaica, but many were already ill and most died. The second wave came in 1864-70, and was 200 persons from Trinidad and British Guiana. The third wave was 680 direct from China via Hong Kong consisting of 501 men, 105 women, 54 girls and 3 babies. The majority of these immigrants were Hakka people from Tung-Kuan, Wei-yagn and Pao-an in Kwangtung province. In 1905 the government restricted the entry of Chinese immigrants into Jamaica.

A source which provides some historical information is "Adjustment patterns among the Jamaican Chinese" by Andrew W. Lind (*Social and Economic Studies*, Vol. 7, No. 2, pp. 144-64, June 1958). Some of the sources listed in the TNA/PRO by Grannum (see East Indian) also pertain to Chinese, e.g. after the 1870s the Land Board and Emigration Department CO 384-386 and CO 428 registers. CO 384-385 includes emigrant ships' registers which sometimes detail births and deaths. Another very personal account is that of Helen Chinsee whose father-in-law is the topic of "A Chinese in Jamaica" by Helen Chinsee (*Jamaica Journal*, Vol. 2, No. 1, pp. 10-14, 1968).

From the Gleaner on line, Out of Many Cultures, The People who came: The Chinese is at: http://www.jamaica-gleaner.com/pages/history/ story0055.htm

Syrians – Lebanese

The 1943 census of Jamaica lists 835 Syrian and 171 Syrian Coloured in the island. These immigrants came to Jamaica in the late nineteenth century to escape oppression from the Muslim Turks and to seek their fortune. Most actually came to the island from Lebanon, but because at that time Lebanon was known as Syria, they are known in Jamaica as Syrians. Lebanese immigrants were mainly Greek Orthodox Christians. Many of their vital records are recorded in Anglican churches since there was no Greek Orthodox Church in Jamaica. Later those immigrants from Bethlehem and Syria proper became Roman Catholic. Several became established merchants in the island; among the names are Issa, Matalon and Hanna.

A short article on this immigration and some of the people involved is "They came from the Middle East" by Nellie Ammar (*Jamaica Journal*, Vol. 4, No. 1, pp. 2-6, March 1970). Nellie's father, Shehadie Khaleel Melick, was one of the immigrants. He became known in Jamaica as Mr. Khaleel, because of the practice the first immigrants used of not using their surnames. Often the second name was that of the father. Nellie Ammar says that most of the very earliest immigrants came from the small town of Schweifat in Lebanon.

There is from Pieces in the Past: in the Daily Gleaner on line entitled Out of Many Cultures, The people who came: The Lebanese: http://www.jamaica-gleaner.com/pages/history/story0056.htm

There are other immigrants who came to Jamaica, but not in such large groups as the above mentioned, so their records and history are more difficult to determine. In the 1844 census, 480 Americans, 331 Spaniards and 225 South American born people were counted. Some Portuguese from the Azores were recruited for work on the plantations after emancipation. Some Spaniards came to Jamaica from Spanish colonies. Other West Indian islands contributed to the diversity which is reflected in the Jamaican motto "Out of many, one people".

Naturalization

Because most of the non-slave immigrants coming to Jamaica were from the United Kingdom, it was not necessary to have papers of naturalization since Jamaica was a British Colony until 1962. However there were exceptions. These included Jews and foreign Protestants as well as French immigrants from Haiti. One source of early naturalizations of Jews is M. S. Giuseppi, editor, *Naturalizations of Foreign Protestants in the American and West Indian Colonies (Pursuant to Statute 13 George II, c7)* (Original published by The Publications of the Huguenot Society of London, 1921. Reprinted Baltimore: Maryland, Genealogical Publishing Co. Inc., 1995, 196 pp., ISBN 0-8063-0157-0). In spite of its name, this list of naturalizations becomes of interest to those researching in Jamaica because it covers 152 Jews and nine foreign Protestants who were naturalized in Jamaica between June 1740 and May 1751. This occupies the first six pages of the book, and the rest deals with naturalizations in America, mainly in Pennsylvania. The country of origin is not given in the book, but the original PRO records may have additional data. This book is also available on microfilm through the Mormon Family History Centers. Look in the FHL Catalog under Jamaica/Naturalization for the microfilm number to order.

The other source of naturalizations is the patent records. (See Land and Patents.) The taking out of a patent was a costly undertaking (I think I have read £10 somewhere), so some people may not have gone through the procedure. I have only looked at a few alphabetical lists of the indexes to patents, for the letters D, G, H, L, Q and W. I extracted the following Patents of Naturalization in the Volumes I, II indexes. Please note this list is by no means complete. These names caught my eye for reasons that they belonged to family or friends.

Year	Name	Naturalization	Vol.	Folio (Page)
1808	Duquesney, Phillipe de Mercier	Naturalization	38	17
1808	Duverger, Jean, B. G.	Naturalization	38	247
1808	Duquesnay, M. C. J.	Naturalization	38	289
1683	Gautier, Ezachariah	Naturalization	10	128
1689	Gaultier, David	Naturalization	12	169
1713	Gabaudon, Stephen	Naturalization	16	148
1759	Hall, John	Naturalization	29	37
1799	Hall, John	Naturalization	37	12
1808	Levy, Judith	Naturalization	38	50
1808	Levy, Moses Snr.	Naturalization	38	228
1808	Levy, Elizabeth	Naturalization	38	250
1808	Levy, Michael	Certificate	38	295

The year 1808 seemed to have been a big year for naturalizations, at least from this record. Naturalizations began in the late 1600s. The two John Hall listings surprised me, but I did not look up the actual patents to see if it told from where he came. The others appear to be French (some émigrés from Haiti) and Jews. The patent records stop in about 1828, so I am not sure at this time where the records of later naturalizations may be found, possibly in deeds or court records. Unfortunately patent records have not been filmed so you will have to employ a records researcher or go to the Spanish Town repositories yourself.

A short list of Jews who were Naturalized in 1743 is listed at: http://www.awesomegenealogy.com/jamaica_jewsnat31may1743.shtml Patricia Jackson on her site has a page with information on Naturalization taken from the Jamaica Handbook of 1891/2 at: http://jamaicanfamilysearch.com/Samples/handbk15.htm. This quotes the Act 35 of Charles II as the basis of Naturalization and details the process.

Emigration

Our ancestors also left the island of Jamaica after establishing homes there. While the biggest emigration is probably in the second half of the twentieth century, since 1655 there have been immigrations outwards. This section is based primarily on my experiences tracking my families. There are some areas of which I have little knowledge, principally emigration to other West Indian islands, which should be considered as a possibility. The other thing to keep in mind is that sometimes people left for work in other countries and later returned to Jamaica. I am not sure that these should be counted as true emigrants since they did not intend to remain elsewhere permanently. Such was the experience of my maternal grandfather, who worked in Detroit Michigan, Costa Rica and Cuba, but he never moved his family to those places. Others of his era, however, married in those countries and had children. My paternal grandfather worked in St. Kitts for about eight years and my father was born there, but the family moved back to Jamaica in the 1920s. This means that finding the records of their lives during that time may involve searching the records of other islands or countries.

American East Coast 1655-1776

I did not realize that there was considerable traffic between Jamaica and the East Coast of America, from the time that Jamaica became a colony in 1655 up until the American Revolution. I had always thought of it the other way, that is people left from England maybe via America to the West Indies. However, in a will proved in Boston 1674, I learned that the writer of the will fully expected his son-in-law, who was a planter in St. Elizabeth, Jamaica, to come to Boston to execute his will. In the event that the son-in-law was not able to come for a certain time he did leave provision with a friend for his wife's benefit, but he fully expected his son-in-law to be able to be there. This means that he knew there were ships which would be coming from the West Indies to Boston. The will was proved in the following year, indicating that the son-in-law was able to get there.

Another family had part of the family in Boston, part in England and part in Jamaica. Letters between these members and the places of birth indicate that there was considerable traffic between the three places in the 1700s. Another family, also of St. Elizabeth, had the daughter marry into the Middleton family of South Carolina and there are letters in Charleston from this daughter mentioning her father, who died in Jamaica in 1793. She was born in Jamaica and the family had been there since 1677. So even after the Revolutionary War there was interaction with the U.S. mainland. Various histories do tell that during the Revolutionary War provision ships from America were cut off, which obliged the estate owners to find a means of providing staples such as corn for the slaves, so they increased provision grounds, because they could not rely on the ships from England reaching Jamaica in time. This suggested that up to that time regular commerce was conducted between Jamaica and the East Coast of America, and even commercial ships would carry one to two passengers. Accounts of the Darien expedition also bear this statement out, because those who left went back to Scotland via New York.

Gold Rush – California and Australia 1849-1900

Gold rushes in the latter half of the nineteenth century drew people from all over the world, and Jamaica was not an exception. What is interesting is how they got there, and how few found what they were seeking, i.e. to get rich. The 1849 gold rush of California drew my great-grandfather from Jamaica. He apparently left Jamaica in 1849/1850 and went to New Orleans, where he is recorded in the 1851 census. Then he took a ship to Panama and crossed the isthmus before there was a canal. At Panama City he took the ship *New Orleans* to Acapulco and then to San Francisco. His arrival there, with lady (his wife) is recorded in a San Francisco newspaper which has been extracted by L. Rasmussen and indexed in Filby's *Ship Passenger List Indexes*. The original records of ships' passengers to San Francisco were destroyed by fire. Advertisements in the *Panama City Star* (the local newspaper) are listed for the ship *New Orleans* sailing to San Francisco. A book which describes the reverse trip, i.e. from San Francisco to Panama City and across the isthmus back to New York, is *The World Rushed In: The California Gold Rush Experience* by J. S. Holliday (New York, Simon and Schuster, 1983, 559 pp., ISBN 0671-25538-X Pbk.), which chronicles the journey of a New Yorker across America to San Francisco and his return trip via Panama without achieving his gold.

My great-grandfather soon moved from San Francisco to San Andreas, Calaveras County, but apparently the gold was all dug out, because with his brother-in-law he was in a merchant business in San Andreas in 1860, and bought 100 feet in a copper mine in Campo Seco, which he sold in 1864. He died in San Francisco in 1872 and is buried in the Home of Peace Cemetery in San Mateo County. Looking at census records (San Francisco, 1852; Calaveras County, 1860; San Francisco 1870), one can see the origins of people from all over the world, including Jamaica; some were black, some mulatto and some white. The 1860 census is very interesting because it lists people's assets in ready cash. Many returned to Jamaica, but some died in California. Some, like the New Yorker in *The World Rushed In*, definitely did return home. In the piece noted below on Australia, a discouraging editorial quotation of the *Falmouth Post* newspaper is that many Jamaicans who had gone to California returned to Jamaica bankrupt.

There were other ways to get to California from the East and from England and the United Kingdom. They included ships from New York, around South America and up the West Coast to San Francisco, and obviously from New Orleans across Panama. So making the westward trip across America by wagon was not the only route. If emigrants stayed in California until 1868, they could have returned to the East Coast by railway, since the transcontinental railway opened in that year; or gone to New Orleans via a train to St. Louis and then by boat down the Mississippi. Other gold rushes could have drawn them on.

One such is the Australian gold rush, which started when gold was discovered in New South Wales in 1851. Jamaicans left in 1852, some via Panama and some around the cape. An article which reveals something of these emigrants and why they left Jamaica and what they met in Australia is "Jamaicans in the Australian Gold Rushes" by Barry Higman (*Jamaica Journal*, Vol. 10, Nos. 2, 3, 4, pp. 38-45, 1976). In the Australian gold rush most of the people leaving Jamaica were white or fair, and they left because of the decline in sugar fortunes in the island. Most black people recently liberated from slavery could not afford the 15-40 pound sterling fare for a passage to Australia.

Gold rushes in Idaho, Montana and Alaska at the end of the century probably drew others as adventurers, but I have not seen any reports of

Jamaicans leaving the island for these opportunities, most of which did not result in fortunes being made.

Panama, Cuba and Costa Rica

In the late nineteenth century and at the beginning of the twentieth century, the building of the Panama Canal and railway drew Jamaican workers to the isthmus. The Jamaicans were highly regarded as adapted to the climate and more resistant to the scourge yellow fever which decimated the American and European workers. Jamaicans viewed it as a way to earn money to return home. Since it was a finite project, the intention was not to emigrate permanently. But there were a few who married and settled there. It is estimated that of the 84,000 persons who left the island, 62,000 returned to Jamaica. The climate was unhealthy for even the Jamaicans, and many did die building the canal. Panama also drew some Jamaican merchants, and judging from the reports of vital records in the *Daily Gleaner* in the early 1900s they had settled permanently there.

Two articles which describe the Panama experience are the two parts of "The Colon People" by Olive Senior in the *Jamaica Journal*: Part 1, "Jamaica the Neglected Garden" (Vol. 11, Nos. 3 & 4, pp. 62-71, 1977), and Part 2, "The Colon Experience: The Panama Canal" (Vol. 12, No. 42, pp. 88-103, 1978/79). A book of West Indian migration to Panama was published in 2004. It is *The Silver Men: West Indian Labour Migration to Panama 1850-1914* by Velma Newton Kingston: Ian Randle Publishers 2004, 244 pp. ISBN 976-637-132-6. As seen by the title this includes other West Indians as well as Jamaicans.

A visit to Panama in 1912 before the canal was opened was chronicled by my maternal great grandfather and is on my website at: http://www.rootsweb.com/~jamwgw/panama.htm

On the other hand, cane and bananas were the work which drew Jamaicans to Cuba and Costa Rica from 1905 to the 1920s. The United Fruit Company, an American company, established banana plantations in Costa Rica, and since they were already established in Jamaica, the opportunities were well known by Jamaicans searching for jobs. Again these were not usually regarded as permanent emigrations although they stayed there for several years, some with their families, some marrying in those places and their children being born there. Mention of this is important so that too much time is not wasted trying to track down records in Jamaica, when the records needed may be from Panama, Cuba or Costa Rica.

England

The 1950s started the new emigration of Jamaicans to England. Most who left during this time, for economic reasons, were skilled or semi-skilled workers or craftsmen, carpenters, masons, etc. Many settled in and near London and Birmingham. Most of them sent money home to support their families and many relatives then joined them in England. After independence in 1962, the emigrants were predominantly expatriates, former colonial workers who retired to Britain and students who did not return to Jamaica. Since many Jamaicans no longer qualified for a British passport, permission to emigrate declined.

Many who emigrated in the 1950s and 1960s, when they first went to Britain, had the idea of working and then retiring to Jamaica. While the Jamaican government encouraged this and made it possible for people to buy land and houses, many changed their minds with the changing economics and political status of Jamaica, and now live permanently in England. The health and social benefits they enjoy in Britain would be lost and not compensated for in Jamaica. Still, there is encouragement to return to Jamaica for retirement.

Canada and the United States

Among Jamaicans emigrating to the United States in the early 1900s are many members of my extended family. They mainly came for economic reasons or for education and then stayed. The peak in emigration to America for all immigrants during this time was 1906. American ships' passenger lists and immigration and naturalization records are probably the best source for tracking emigrants for this era. The Ellis Island immigration records are the best source if they entered the US or Canada through New York. The on-line site for searching these records is: http://www.ellisislandrecords.org/. You may also find on this site when people visited the United States from Jamaica rather than emigrate.

I do not know of any sources of emigration records in Jamaica. In the 1920s and '30s some passengers leaving Jamaica by ship, and later by plane, are listed in the *Daily Gleaner*, but there is no index, so no way of readily accessing this potential source.

In the latter part of the twentieth century, immigration to North America has held a great attraction for Jamaicans. It was often more possible to obtain papers to enter Canada, and many Jamaicans settled in Ontario or British Columbia. In the United States the settlements were spread out, but during the Manley era (1970s) many emigrated to Florida, especially Tampa and Miami. New York, Boston and Los Angeles also have a fair number of Jamaicans who formed the exodus from Jamaica at this time. Many feared the rise of communism and the social democratic movement, which involved government takeover of private business, e.g. bauxite, utilities, etc. So they withdrew capital from Jamaica, which started a decline in the quality of life, which induced even more people to leave. Some seasonal sugar cane and vegetable workers were employed in Florida and Louisiana, but these would come to the U.S. for 6-8 months and then return to Jamaica.

The desire to emigrate to America can be shown in the year I emigrated, 1969. In that year 18,000 Jamaicans applied for and received permanent visas. At that time there was a quota for the western hemisphere of 175,000 people. Jamaica, which had 1% of the population of the western hemisphere, had 10% of the applications for permanent visas that year. That is why it took me nine months to obtain my visa, even though I had a job guaranteed at a university. Passports, immigration papers and naturalization certificates are the likely sources of documenting these emigrants.

Since 1980, some emigrants have drifted back to Jamaica, or they maintain homes in both places. I have not heard of large numbers of retirees returning to Jamaica, but that was the goal of many who left Jamaica in the 1960s for Canada and America.

Military Records

During the seventeenth and eighteenth centuries, Britain was usually at war with either Spain or France, and the Caribbean often featured in these wars, because various islands were colonies of each participant. In order to protect their island from attack from another country, all Jamaican landowners in the island from the very earliest times had to agree to bear arms, provide their own weapons and horses and join the militias which were organized by parish. Militias existed at least up to emancipation and even to the time of the Morant Bay Rebellion in 1865. Beginning before the American Revolutionary War, various regiments of the British Army were stationed in the island, and they continued to be up until independence in 1962. They were called upon to fight in the First and Second Maroon Wars up to the late 1790s, but apart from that they never fought battles on Jamaican soil. Nonetheless they were there to put down rebellions of slaves and to protect the island from foreign invaders if they came. The Navy and Royal Artillery were also stationed in the island, mainly at Port Royal. Lord Nelson as a young naval officer was stationed there and today there is a plaque in Fort Charles at Port Royal to his memory.

At the beginning of the nineteenth century, the British Army began to recruit men of Jamaica and other West Indian islands for the British West India Regiments (12 in all), which were abandoned in the twentieth century (1927). During WWI and WWII, men from Jamaica volunteered and served in the forces in these wars on the side of the Allies and Britain. Records from military sources exist for nearly all these military pursuits, most of them in the TNA/PRO in London.

Militia

The militia was an obligation of all white settlers (and later free people of colour) of Jamaica from early times. They had to be ready to supply arms and horses and muster when an alarm was raised for threats either internally or externally. The militia was organized in the early 1800s in the following manner. Each county (Cornwall, Middlesex and Surrey) had a regiment of horse, with troops one from each parish in the county. In addition, each parish had a foot regiment. Thus you will see in the *Jamaica Almanacks* e.g. 1824, lists of officers from the Middlesex Regiment of Horse, St. Ann Troop, and from a St. Ann Regiment of Foot. I have been unable to find any sources of lists of the ordinary men of the militia, which would be a valuable type of census of landowners at various times. The Spanish Town Archives reports that it does not hold any such records. As mentioned above, some names of officers are reported in the *Jamaica Almanac*s by parish. This information can be seen on Patricia Jackson's site at: http://jamaicanfamilysearch.com/ Members/Almanacs.htm This site has some free pages, but to obtain the full advantage of the information you need to subscribe. The fees are very reasonable, for example in 2006 the cost was $8.00US for 1 month. I wonder if any vestry minutes of parishes have any militia lists since this was a function at the parish level. A good description of the militia organization is included in *The Development of the Creole Society in Jamaica, 1770-1820* by E. Braithwaite (Oxford: Clarendon Press, 1971, 374 pp.).

American Revolutionary War Units

During the American Revolutionary War there were several units which the British Army sent to Jamaica or raised in Jamaica. These are listed in the book *Encyclopedia of British, Provincial and German Army Units, 1775-1783* by Philip Katcher (Harrisburg, Pennsylvania: The Stackpole Co., 1973, 160 pp.). A book which I used to confirm these is *In Search of the "Forlorn Hope": a Comprehensive Guide to Locating British Regiments and Their Records (1640-WWI)* by John M. Kitzmiller II (Salt Lake City, Utah: Manuscript Publishing Foundation, 3 vols., 1988). Kitzmiller does not address the provincial units, and he lists additional units which were in Jamaica during the American Revolutionary War, 1775-1783 (Volume I, Chapter VI).

Those sent to Jamaica included (from Katcher's *Encyclopedia*):

1. **3rd Regiment of Foot.** (The Buffs) Now the 1st Battalion/The Queen's Regiment. Sent to Jamaica from Charleston in December 1782. Kitzmiller confirms they were in Jamaica 1782-83.

2. **14th Regiment of Foot.** Now the Prince of Wales' own Regiment of Yorkshire. Sent to Jamaica after being reformed in England and arrived there in April 1782. Kitzmiller has the dates 1782-85 for this regiment in Jamaica.

3. **79th Regiment of Foot.** (Royal Liverpool Volunteers, Liverpool Blues) 1100 men were raised in Liverpool in January 1778, sent to Jamaica in March 1779. Some were sent on to Honduras and Nicaragua in February 1780. Only 84 men returned to Liverpool in February 1784 and were disbanded there. Kitzmiller lists that they were in Jamaica in 1780 and in 1782-83.

4. **85th Regiment of Foot.** (Westminster Volunteers) Raised in Westminster in July 1779 and sent to Jamaica in 1780. Returned to Westminster and disbanded in 1783. Kitzmiller records the 85th as being at Up Park Camp (Kingston) in 1780-82.

5. **92nd Regiment of Foot.** Was raised in England in July 1779 and sent to Jamaica in March 1780. Returned to England and was disbanded there in 1783. In 1780 and again in 1782, Kitzmiller records the 92nd was in Jamaica.

6. **94th Regiment of Foot.** Was raised in England in July 1779 and sent to Jamaica in February 1780. Returned to England and was disbanded there in 1783. Kitzmiller records this regiment was in Jamaica in 1780 and 1782.

7. Provincial Units: **Amherst's Corps.** Was raised in New York and Charleston in 1780 and sent to Jamaica, where it was merged with the Loyal American Rangers or the Duke of Cumberland's Regiment.

8. Provincial Units: **Duke of Cumberland's Regiment.** Was raised in Charleston in February 1781. Six companies (4 officers and 94 men each) were sent to Jamaica in August 1781 and spent the war there. Disbanded 24 August 1783 and the men settled in Nova Scotia.

9. Provincial Units: **Loyal American Rangers.** Was raised in New York in 1780 from prisoners and deserters. Sent to Kingston, Jamaica in February 1781 and then to Pensacola, but returned to Jamaica when they heard Pensacola had fallen. Some 80 men were

sent to Honduras in August 1782. Merged with the Duke of Cumberland's Regiment (see above #8) in January 1783.

10. Provincial Units: **Maryland Loyalists.** Formed in Philadelphia in 1777, this unit returned with the Army to New York in 1778. It was sent to Halifax in September 1778 and on to Jamaica in December 1778. From there it was sent to Pensacola in January 1779, where it served until Pensacola fell in May 1781. Taken prisoner, they were sent to Havana, Cuba, for a month and then paroled to New York. Then they were exchanged for Spanish prisoners in July 1782 and spent the remainder of the war on garrison duty in New York. They were disbanded in New Brunswick.

The encyclopedia gives more detail than given here with respect to the dress and to the commanders of the units.

What is obvious from the foregoing is that units of British and American soldiers spent from one month to four years in Jamaica during the American war, and during that time may have married or had children with Jamaicans. They may also have been recruited into other units, because there were one regiment and several provincial units raised in Jamaica according to the same source.

These units included:

11. **99th (Jamaica) Regiment of Foot.** Raised in Jamaica in 1780 where it did garrison duty until disbanded there in 1784. Kitzmiller confirms that this regiment was in Jamaica 1780-84.

12. Provincial Units: **Independent Companies.** Raised in Jamaica in 1780, with one captain, one lieutenant, one ensign, three sergeants, three corporals, two drummers and 40 privates. The first company commander was Captain Edward Davis. And the second company commanders were Captain Park and Captain William Ross Darby. This unit was merged with the Loyal American Rangers (see above #9) in 1781.

13. Provincial Units: **Jamaica Legion.** Raised in Jamaica in the fall of 1779 and sent on the invasion of Honduras and Nicaragua in February 1780. It was merged with the Jamaica Volunteers in October 1780. The commander was Major John Dalrymple and it had 213 men in four companies.

14. Provincial Units: **Jamaica Volunteers.** Raised in the fall of 1779 and had the same history as the Jamaica Legion (see above #13) and then was merged with the Jamaica Legion and the Royal Batteaux Men (see below #15) in February 1780. The commander

was Major John Macdonald and the strength was 258 men in five companies. This unit was disbanded in Jamaica in April 1781.

15. Provincial Units: **Royal Batteaux Men.** Raised in Jamaica in the fall of 1779 and had the same history as the Jamaica Volunteers (see above #14). Its commander was Colonel Alexander Leith, BT.

There was also a black unit raised in Jamaica. This unit:

16. Provincial Units: **Jamaica Rangers.** A negro corps raised in Jamaica in the fall of 1779 which had three battalions, commanded by 1st Major William Henry Ricketts, 2nd Major William Lewis and 3rd Major Nathaniel Beckford. Each battalion had one major, six captains, one captain-lieutenant, seven lieutenants, eight ensigns, one chaplain, one adjutant, one quartermaster, one surgeon and two mates, 24 sergeants, 24 corporals, 16 drummers and 376 privates. The 3rd battalion was formed in October 1782. Katcher did not know the ultimate disposition of this unit or when it was disbanded, and it is not mentioned in books about the British West India regiments. Nor could I find reference to pensions paid to any of these units. Kitzmiller does not treat provincial units such as these; however some of these records are in the TNA/PRO Kew (see Readers' Guide #11).

Some articles on Provincial and Volunteer Corps are found in the RCS library. They include: "Jamaican Provincial Corps, 1780-1783" by A. W. Haarman (*J. Army Historical Research Society*, Vol. 48, No. 193, pp. 8-13, 1970), and "The Jamaican Volunteer Corps, 1779-1781" (*American Historical Research Journal*, Vol. 49, No. 200, pp. 249-250, 1971).

English Regiments

As mentioned above, many British Army units were located in Jamaica from the 1655 conquest up to independence. The early regiments are hard to define, since the British Army did not have regular designations until the eighteenth century; rather the units were named for their commanders. Thus the army of Penn and Venables who conquered Jamaica was in different units. I have not been able to find a source for these units or other units which were brought to Jamaica by the early military leaders.

After the organization in the Army, units were assigned to the island to help with the defense from chiefly Spanish and French invaders, but also internal strife such as the Maroon Wars. There appear to be three major times when there was a build up of units in Jamaica: the First Maroon War in 1739-42, the American Revolution, and the Second

Maroon War in 1794-8. In order to keep the Maroons in check, barracks were built in the interior of the island. A 1765 map taken from Browne's *History of Jamaica* shows the locations of many but not all of the barracks. Some articles on certain barracks can be found in the *Jamaica Journal*, e.g. "The Stony Hill Barracks" by David Buisseret (*Jamaica Journal*, Vol. 7, Nos. 1 & 2, pp. 22-24, 1973).

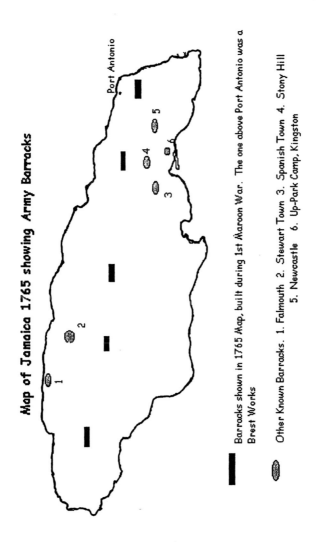

Map of Jamaica 1765 showing Army Barracks

Barracks shown in 1765 Map, built during 1st Maroon War. The one above Port Antonio was a Brest Works

Other Known Barracks. 1. Falmouth 2. Stewart Town 3. Spanish Town 4. Stony Hill 5. Newcastle 6. Up-Park Camp, Kingston

The regimental tabulation given below is an extraction I did from selected parishes of the births, deaths and marriages where a regiment was mentioned. It is only a clue, because I did not do a systematic search of all parishes, only those where I had a family interest. The table does at least indicate that the regiment was there long enough for the event to take place. Sometimes the commanding officer is mentioned as giving permission for marriages.

Regiments located in Jamaica
in the Eighteenth and Nineteenth Centuries
("Extracted from Parish records of Baptisms, Burials and Marriages"
by Madeleine Mitchell)

Year	Regiment	Parish in which located
1796	20th Light Dragoons	Trelawny
1796	83rd Regiment	Trelawny
1797	83rd Regiment	Trelawny
1799	83rd Regiment	Trelawny
1801	60th Regiment, 1st Batt	Trelawny
1802	55th Regiment	Westmoreland
1803	55th Regiment	Trelawny
1807	54th Regiment	St. Andrew
1807	55th Regiment	St. Andrew
1808	18th Royal Irish Regiment	St. Andrew
1809	60th Regiment, 1st Batt	Trelawny
1810	18th Regiment	St. Andrew
1810	60th Regiment, 6th Batt	St. Andrew
1812	101st Regiment	Trelawny
1812	York Light Infantry	St. Andrew
1813	101st Regiment	St. Andrew
1813	18th Regiment	Trelawny
1813	York Light Infantry Volunteer	Trelawny
1815	85th Regiment	St. Andrew
1816	60th Regiment, 6th Batt	Trelawny
1817	20th Light Dragoons	St. Andrew
1817	58th Regiment	St. Andrew
1817	61st Regiment	St. Andrew
1819	50th Regiment	St. Andrew
1820	92nd Regiment	St. Andrew
1821	58th Regiment	St. Andrew

Year	Regiment	Parish in which located
1821	61st Regiment	Trelawny
1822	33rd Regiment	St. Andrew
1823	2nd Regiment	Trelawny
1823	92nd Regiment	Trelawny
1824	33rd Regiment	Trelawny
1824	33rd Regiment	Westmoreland
1824	77th Regiment	St. Andrew

A further listing such as this may be seen in Patricia Jackson's list of Military records in Jamaica. She has compiled them from Anglican and Roman Catholic Registers, Almanacs and newspapers. These are subsciption pages, but the fees are very modest, e.g. in 2006 it costs $8.00 US for a month. http://jamaicanfamilysearch.com/Members/Military.htm

For Book sources, a more complete compilation of regimental locations is given in *In Search of the "Forlorn Hope": A Comprehensive Guide to Locating British Regiments and Their Records (1640-WWI)* by John M. Kitzmiller II (Salt Lake City, Utah: Manuscript Publishing Foundation, 3 vols., 1988). These records can lead you to documents for soldiers and officers in the regiment, but you do need to know the regiment for locating records in the TNA/PRO and FHLibrary. This list at least allows you to narrow the scope of the search if you know the year your ancestor was in Jamaica.

On-line Patricia Jackson has lists of regiments in Jamaica at her site: http://jamaicanfamilysearch.com/Members/Military.htm. This page also leads to lists of Soldiers and Seaman in Jamaican records. There are many excellent books on British military records to consult for establishing an army connection, e.g. TNA/PRO guides, SoG publications. For a discussion see Guy Grannum, *Tracing Your West Indian Ancestors: Sources in the Public Record Office.*

Documents for WWI have just recently been released in Britain. Unfortunately much of the collection was destroyed in WWII in bombing in Exeter, where records had been sent for safekeeping. Some however do remain and are being transferred to the TNA/PRO Kew. F. Cundall made a list of commissioned officers who served as well as an obituary list of Jamaican officers and men who died in WWI. It is found, in appendix lists and pp. 105-121, in *Jamaica's Part in the Great War, 1914-1918: with a foreword by Brevet-Colonel Herbert Bryan* by Frank Cundall (London: West India Committee, 1925, 155 pp.). This book is available in the FHLibrary, and is also available on microfiche, but has not been microfilmed. WWII documents are generally publicly not available, but next of kin can apply to regimental offices in Britain for information. Grannum lists some battalion WWII war diaries which are available in the TNA/PRO.

Navy and Royal Artillery

The British Navy was also in Jamaica, stationed at Port Royal, headed by an admiral. A navy hospital was at Greenwich Hospital, shown in early maps near the Hunt's Bay road on the Kingston side of the harbour. Nelson was for a time assigned to Port Royal, and a plaque and location called Nelson's Quarter Deck are a stop on the local sites to see in Port Royal. One should not however limit inquiry to Port Royal; Kingston should also be included. The Kingston parish church is the site of Admiral Benbow's monumental inscription, and other naval personnel may be buried married or christened there.

The Royal Artillery were also located at Port Royal and their records in births, deaths and marriages in Port Royal Anglican parish records are quite frequent. This can particularly be seen as the abbreviation RA listed after the name.

Additional records (in addition to parish records) for both of these groups reside in the TNA/ PRO at Kew in London. A source to begin searching for these relatives is Chapter 6 in *Tracing Your West Indian Ancestors: Sources in the Public Record Office* by Guy Grannum (Public Record Office Readers' Guide No. 11, London: PRO Publications, 2nd Edition, 2002, 194 pp., ISBN 903365 38 4). As for the Army, this readers' guide locates the pertinent documents for the Navy and Royal Artillery. Additional pamphlet guides are available from the Public Record Office.

Port Royal was also the location of the major dockyard for the Navy, and records for Jamaica exist. They include admiralty musters and pay lists up until the mid-nineteenth century. Again reference numbers for these in the Public Record Office may be obtained from *Tracing Your West Indian Ancestors* by Guy Grannum. Some pension records may be available. There may have been dockyards for merchant ships at other ports in Jamaica, e.g. Falmouth, Port Antonio, Sav-la-Mar, but I have not found any reference material to them at this time.

West India Regiments

The West India Regiments deserve a special note. The men were originally drawn from ex-slaves who served in the American

Revolutionary War, mainly from South Carolina. They were very controversial with the Army authorities and with the white planters in the islands who did not approve of arming black men. The early regiments therefore had white officers. But the climate of the tropics drove the Army to build up 12 regiments called the West India Regiments. I gather that the 2nd Regiment was the one most associated with Jamaica, but other units may have served there at one time or another. See Patricia Jackson's site. In 1807 when importation of slaves from Africa to the West Indies was prohibited, slave ships caught trading had their slaves confiscated and many of the slaves were sold to the British Army for the West India regiments. A real conflict between government departments' behaviour, one would have thought. Why were they not taken back to Africa? I suppose cost of return transportation is one factor, but in my mind that does not fully explain this peculiar behaviour. Some slaves may have thought the Army led to greater opportunities than the plantations; however, since their units were located in some of the worst geographical areas for disease, the losses of life must not have been that different than on the estates.

Records for the West India regiments may also be found in Chapter 6 of *Tracing Your West Indian Ancestors* by Guy Grannum (Public Record Office Readers' Guide No. 11, London: PRO Publications, 2002, 194 pp., ISBN 1-903365-38-4). These include muster and pay lists, pension registers, description books, casualty returns and soldiers' documents, some covering the period 1760-1888. Some pension records continue to 1903. Casualty returns may contain wills or copies of wills.

A history of the early constitution of the West India Regiments is found in *Slaves in Red Coats: The British West India Regiments, 1795-1815* by Roger N. Buckley (London and New Haven, Connecticut, U.S.: Yale University Press, 1979, 210 pp., ISBN 0-300-02216-6). This book indicates that most regiments were disbanded after the Napoleonic Wars, but they were resurrected later and finally disbanded in 1927 at least in Jamaica, except for the band, which with its distinctive uniform is featured in many post cards and books up to later in the twentieth century. Some of the officers who volunteered in WWI were located in the British West India Regiments, (This latter statement is based on obituaries in the *Daily Gleaner* from that period.) World War I battalion war diaries and Medal lists are reported in Grannum, *Tracing your West Indian Ancestors*. A revolt by the British West India Regiment in 1918 in Italy is described in "Revolt of the British West India Regiment" by W. F. Elkins (*Jamaica Journal*, Vol. 11, Nos. 3 & 4, pp. 73-75, 1977). After the war a technical school was set up for disabled veterans of the British

West India Regiment. This report is in the RCS library, entitled: "Technical School for disabled men of the British West Indies Regiment, report for period form 1st August 1917 to 31st March 1918." [*Jamaican Reports*] V. Kingston.

Information about the British West India Regiments is at: http://website.lineone.net/~bwir/ with more history of the WWI British West Indian Regiment at http://website.lineone.net/~bwir/bwi_regt.htm. Another page on this site leads to information particularly of Jamaica including the site for the current Jamaica Defense Force site. Look at the bottom of the first URL page listed in this paragraph. Men of the second contingent sent from Jamaica to England in WWI are listed on my site at: http://www.rootsweb.com/~jamwgw/contin.htm. A description of the ill-fated third contingent is also on this site http://www.rootsweb.com/~jamwgw/3contin.htm. Officers of many of the contingents are listed on Patricia Jackson's site.

See also Jamaica Almanacs for Military Lists (Officers only)

Schools, Colleges and University

In general, school records of pupils do not appear to have been kept until the late nineteenth and twentieth centuries. For this reason, I have not done extensive research in this area and other sources should be consulted e.g. Ingram's *Bibliography of Jamaica*. However, most of the latter references are of the twentieth century rather than historical. Ingram's *Sources of Jamaican History* does list for earlier times (p. 544) some manuscript sources of free school minutes in the Jamaica Archives, Institute of Jamaica and British Library. These may include some lists of pupils (see below).

Early settlers from England sent their sons, but rarely their daughters, to the "home" country to be educated if they could afford it. So early English public school records may contain some information on prominent families. Lady Nugent in the early 1800s considered many of the Creole white men and women to be very poorly educated, indicating there were not many opportunities for Jamaican-born whites to obtain education in Jamaica, especially for women. Some references which contain information on the history of education in Jamaica include C. Campbell, "Social and economic obstacles to the development of popular education in post-emancipation Jamaica, 1834-1865" (*Journal of Caribbean History*, Vol. 1, pp. 57-88, 1970), and Millicent Whyte, *A Short History of education in Jamaica* (London: Hodder & Stoughton, 1977, 128 pp.), used as a training reference at Mico. Various colonial administration reports, e.g. the Lumb Report of 1898, are reviewed in *Reports and Repercussions in West Indian education 1835-1933* by Shirley C. Gordon (Kingston: Caribbean Universities Press, 1968, 190 pp.).

Free Schools

One of the first references I saw to a school was to the free school established by a will of Charles Drax, who owned a plantation in St. Ann, near St. Ann's Bay. His will took a long time in being settled, but the money set aside for a free school established the school at Walton Pen in St. Ann. Quoting in part from an 1838 almanac of Jamaica, "In 1797, the Justices and Vestry were authorized to raise funds by taxation for the purpose of recovering property of Charles Drax, which he had bequeathed to endow a Free School. In 1802, compromise being effected with his executors and £11,200 recovered in 1807 establishing Walton Pen as the seat of the Jamaica Free School. In 1820 a case in Chancery, Allan Exor vs. Ramsay... the Duke of Manchester then Chancellor gave it ... [to the Vestry]. Of Walton School, the schoolroom is spacious and capable of accommodating to near 100 scholars. The master who must be M.A. has permission to take as many private scholars as he thinks proper" (pp. 81-82). This school later became Jamaica College Boys School now in St. Andrew.

By 1826 there were free schools in the following parishes as gleaned from the 1826 *Jamaica Almanac*:

School	Master	Treasurer
St. Catherines Free School	Mr. George Marcus	John Lunan, Esq.
Vere Free School	Rev. U. G. Rose	John Holmes
St. Ann, at Walton Pen	Rev. Geo. W. Askew	Geo. F. Coward
Kingston, Wolmer's Free School	Mr. Ebenezer Read	Joseph Barnes
Portland, Titchfield Free School	Rev. A. Bunting	Dr. Wm. Arnold
Westmoreland, Mannings Free School		
Hanover, Rusea Free School		
St. James Free School	Rev. Henry Tauton	

As will be noted many of the masters were Anglican curates for the parish and did more than one job. It is not clear how many teachers there were in these free schools, other than the master. It should be noted that these schools were established by the Church of England and the Vestries of the Parish and were exclusively for the (poor) white population at first. After 1814 the Christian free coloured were admitted (see below for Wolmer's). Reading and writing were prohibited for slave populations up to the time of the establishment of these schools. The non-conformists also established schools for the children of slaves; the

Presbyterians established six, the Moravians 12, the Baptists four and the proprietors of estates nine.

The manuscripts mentioned by Ingram in *Sources of Jamaican History* include lists of scholars or boys or accounts for: Wolmer's Free School, Vere Free School, Rusea Free School, Mannings Free School, Walton Free School. The establishment of Spanish Town Free School is confirmed by a donation given to it by Mrs. Bathshua Beckford, wife of Peter Beckford, in 1743.

The Development of the Creole Society in Jamaica, 1770-1820 by E. Braithwaite (Oxford: Clarendon Press, 1971, 374 pp.) also has a section on education in Jamaica prior to emancipation.

Church Schools, e.g. Wolmer's, York Castle

When I went to secondary school in Jamaica in the 1950s, the schools were all church-affiliated although government supported. The earliest secondary school is Wolmer's Boys School which was established in 1729 in Kingston. *Daily Gleaner* announcements from the late 1800s and early 1900s call for meetings of the Old Boys of Wolmer's and meetings of the Board of Trustees. Present-day Jamaica College (boys' secondary school) was in 1895 called Jamaica High School. St. Hilda's High School for Girls (Anglican) was established in 1922, although begun as the Diocesan High School for Girls in 1906 and St. Andrew High School for Girls (Presbyterian) was established in 1925.

At Wolmer's, coloured pupils were admitted first in 1814 and gradually became the majority. The Cambridge University library holds a report on education in 1838. It is entitled "Copy of a Report from C. J. Latrobe on Negro Education in Jamaica" (96 pp., 1838). A table from the report by Latrobe in 1838 gives the following enrollment data for Wolmer's:

Year	White	Coloured
1814	87	-
1815	111	3
1816	129	25
1817	146	36
1818	155	38
1819	136	57
1820	116	78
1821	118	122

Year	White	Coloured
1822	93	167
1823	97	187
1824	94	196
1825	89	185
1826	93	176
1827	92	156
1828	88	152
1829	79	192
1830	88	194
1831	88	315
1832	90	360
1833	93	411
1834	81	420
1835	85	425
1836	78	428
1837	N/A	N/A

This kind of pattern may have been similar in other free schools. In 1838 it was said by Latrobe that "the upper classes scarcely benefit as they are taken away from school too early, as those who can write a tolerable hand and hold a competent knowledge of arithmetic are the traders and merchants of the city".

York Castle Boarding School was established in 1876 by the Methodist Church on the former property of York Castle estate, St. Ann, held by the Sicard family. In fact the Governor of the Theological College associated with this school was my great-grandfather, Rev. William Clarke Murray. One of the first teachers was my paternal grandfather, William Herbert Mitchell, who came out from Bristol, England, to teach mathematics and was later Headmaster at York Castle. The school had many successes as evidenced in the *Handbooks of Jamaica* for 1891-5 when students from York Castle began to win Jamaica Scholarships; by 1894, three of the five Jamaica Scholarships had been won by boys at York Castle. Some of the graduates of York Castle School became leaders in Jamaican life. At the time it was not limited to the white population, but was open to all scholastic achievers. Unfortunately the school did not make it financially and was closed in 1899. (Later the Methodists, under Rev. J. Poxon, reestablished a secondary school called York Castle located in Brown's Town, St. Ann. This is a government supported school now.) An article by F. Cundall in 1911 comments on the history of secondary education In Jamaica. It is entitled "Some notes on the history of secondary education in Jamaica" (in the *Handbook of Jamaica*, 1911, pp. 599-612), and can be found in the RCS library.

If you are an Alumnus/a of a Jamaican secondary school you can list your e-mail address at the following site so that you can contact and be contacted by fellow schoolmates: http://www.pacificnet.net/~jaweb/jaalumni/jaindex.html.

Schools for Freed Slaves

One of the chief goals of the leading emancipators from Britain was to establish schools for the freed slaves after 1834. By 1824 there were 40 schools altogether open for the education of the children of free coloured and ex-slaves, mostly set up by the non-conformists. After denying slaves the access to literacy during the time of slavery, it was deemed necessary to provide access to the skills of reading, writing and arithmetic, and religious instruction so that the former slaves could achieve "civilized" citizenship. So the non-conformist churches were among the first to establish schools in villages of freed slaves. This was, in my understanding, the beginning of primary education in Jamaica. However, these schools were not universal and by the early 1890s something more was considered necessary. Proposals which were debated in the *Daily Gleaner* by the leading ministers of the time in 1891 (*Daily Gleaner*, August 19, 1891) called the Educational Conference shows how far they had come and how far they had to go.

Teachers' Colleges and the University

The non-conformist churches established training schools for the instruction of religious leaders as well as lay teachers. One of the first was the Mico College, still a training college for primary school teachers. A history of this college is found in *The Mico College, Jamaica: some account of the Mico family, the story of the Mico fund, its diversion to the West Indies and its latest developments in Jamaica, with a brief history of the College* by Frank Cundall (Kingston: printed by the Gleaner Co. for the Directors of Mico College, 1914, 98 pp.).

The University of the West Indies at Mona was started in 1948 as a college of the University of London, as well as units at Cave in Barbados and the former Imperial College of Tropical Agriculture in St. Augustine, Trinidad. It was called the University College of the West Indies. Princess Alice was the first chancellor and a stamp was issued in commemoration of the founding. The early professors were all drawn from abroad. After independence in 1962 it became the University of the West Indies with campuses at Mona, Kingston, Jamaica; Cave, Barbados; and St. Augustine, Trinidad. Many Jamaicans have served as the professoriate and as administrators. It is to be hoped that for later generations of genealogists, the records of attendance of students and the employment of the professoriate are well preserved and archived.

Almanacs, Handbooks and Directories

Almanacs, handbooks and directories can add to the lists of persons discussed in an earlier section. But they contribute additional descriptions and information, so are here considered separately. At the beginning of the twentieth century, *Who's Who* began to be published in Jamaica and considerable information on prominent persons is added to this list.

Almanacs

The Jamaica Almanac started as *The Jamaica Almanack* in 1672 and continued into the nineteenth century, up to 1880. K. E. Ingram in his book *Sources of Jamaican History, 1655-1838: A Bibliographical Survey with Particular Reference to Manuscript Sources* (London: Inter Documentation Company, UK Ltd., 1976, 2 vols., 1310 pp.) gives a list of all *Jamaica Almanac*s reported to have been published up to 1838, including for each the year, the full name, the library or repository in which it is located and the source of the information (List G, p. 1042).

At first these almanacs were little more than astronomical and astrological manuals applied to the West Indies. In the late 1700s they started to be published in Jamaica, and information about the land, topography and crops began to be introduced as well as the names of official persons (including pound keepers!). In the nineteenth century they become really useful because in addition to the above, they list proprietors of estates, number of slaves (later apprentices), acreage and sometimes the name of the estate. The years 1811, 1815, 1824, 1826, 1838 and 1840 are particularly of interest for these lists, which are by parish. I have seen all. From the listing of the number of slaves or apprentices, one can judge to some extent the wealth of the family.

In addition to the list given by Ingram, *Jamaica Almanac*s are available in microfilm form at the National Library of Jamaica (Series 1965N-1979N). They cover the years 1677 to 1847 but are not continuous, e.g. there is a gap between 1677 and 1751. Ten reels cover the years 1796 to 1847 where they were published. It would be nice if these were copied and available elsewhere. The 1824, 1826 and 1840 editions are available as books in the library of the Royal Commonwealth Society, Cambridge University Library, Cambridge, England. The 1838 edition is available in the Boston Public Library in the Rare Book section.

Patricia Jackson has done a tremendous job of transcribing most of the Proprietor lists of Almanacs that are available as well as the Civil and Military lists from the Almanacs. Her site is for pay but is very reasonable (for example in 2006 it costs $8.00 US for a month) http://jamaicanfamilysearch.com/

Handbooks

The *Handbooks of Jamaica* took over from where the *Almanac*s left off and carried similar material, e.g. official persons and magistrates. There are yearly volumes from 1881-1939, 1946, 1948, 1950, 1952-55, 1958-59, 1961, 1963-67 and 1971. At least these are the holdings of the library of the Royal Commonwealth Society, Cambridge University Library, Cambridge, England. The FHLibrary, Salt Lake City, has 1890 and 1963.

These handbooks in the late 1890s have information on sugar estates, including such details as their yield, and whether they were water or steam driven. Information is listed by parish, but not every parish is covered. Some parishes no longer grew sugar cane as they had in the eighteenth century. An interesting section of the 1895 *Handbook* carries information on boys who had won the Jamaica Scholarships to that time and on persons who had obtained passes in the Local and Cambridge external examinations, listing the school and headmaster from which they came.

Patricia Jackson at her site has some free pages devoted to the 1891/2, 1900 and 1919 Handbooks. http://jamaicanfamilysearch.com/ Samples/handbook.htm. They include the stations and membership numbers in various denominations in Jamaica, as well as properties in cultivation and their proprietors.

Who's Who

The *Who's Who of Jamaica* began publication in the 20th century, and it has been published sporadically in Kingston since then. Editions are held in the National Library of Jamaica (NLJ), formerly the Institute of Jamaica. The Royal Commonwealth Society Library (Cambridge University Library, Cambridge, England), holds the following editions: 1916 (1st edition), 1921, 1924 (3rd), 1941-46, 1951 (7th), 1954 (8th). These are very useful tools if your ancestor was prominent enough to be a J.P. (Justice of the Peace), businessman, clergy, etc. and was not limited to being an expatriate colonial civil servant, although many of the latter are listed. They often give the names of the father and mother of the person. The 1916 first edition has pictures of people and also lists persons who had recently died, in 1909 for example.

A transcription of the 1916 Who's Who appears on Patricia Jackson's site at:

http://jamaicanfamilysearch.com/Samples2/whoswho.htm

Directories

I have not discovered a run of commercial directories for the island as are seen in England from the 1800s, e.g. Kelly's, Pigot's, nor as found in big cities in the U.S. There are however a couple worth mentioning. One is the *1878 Directory* which lists mainly merchants of Kingston, but also includes other parishes. Establishments like schools, synagogues and churches are also listed. A copy of this directory is found in the National Library of Jamaica.

Another directory which is found in the Royal Commonwealth Society Library (Cambridge University Library, Cambridge, England) is called the *Jamaica Commercial Memorandum Book and Pocket Journal with Almanac for 1891* by Mortimer DeSouza. It lists merchants by parish as well as some pen keepers and clergymen. One amusing entry was a Dr. F. Purchas of Spats-Man-Hole Pen in Trelawny. It was supposed to be Sportsman's Hall Pen, Trelawny. One wonders how the compiler got his information, word of mouth? Or were the printers at fault?

I also found reference in the RCS library to *The Times Commercial Directory of Jamaica, 1910* by H. M. Cornish (Kingston: 247 pp.).

For members, Patricia Jackson's site has copies of the 1878, 1891 and 1910 Directories http://jamaicanfamilysearch.com/ See under directories.

For current residential telephone directories see http://jamaica.jamaicayp.com/whitebook.html. Choose New Search to put in a name. For yellow pages use http://www.yellowpagesjamaica.com/

Courts and Legal Action

When I mentioned to someone that I would include courts and legal action in my book, she said, "Who would want to know if their ancestor was a thief or robber or murderer?" Well, that is not the only information one can glean from examining court records. People may be witnesses, they might have had a dispute about land and property boundaries, the proper heirs might need to be found to a will, and rare divorces may have been sought. There are all sorts of other reasons why lawsuits may have been filed. Another thing to keep in mind is that today's serious crimes are not the serious crimes of yesterday. In England in the 1600-1700s one might have been transported for stealing a shilling or a handkerchief. So the seriousness of the crime in early days in Jamaica may not be what we consider serious crimes today. However, that said, I must confess that I have not examined court records of Jamaica, although I know they exist. They reside in Jamaica in the Archives and Registrar General's Office and have not to my knowledge been copied or microfilmed.

Since Jamaica was a British colony, the law established in Jamaica was based on British law. There appear, from K. E. Ingram's book (pp. 548-554, *Sources of Jamaican History, 1655-1838: A Bibliographical Survey with Particular Reference to Manuscript Sources*, London: Inter Documentation Company, UK Ltd., 1976, 2 vols., 1310 pp.), to be four main courts: the Court of Chancery, the Jamaica Supreme Court, the Jamaica Grand Court or Court of Error, and the Court of the Ordinary. In addition there were Assize Courts held by county or parish, and a few of their records are deposited in the RGO e.g. St. James, Hanover, St. Andrew. The latter courts held quarter sessions and petty sessions. The system also included magistrates in each parish and Justices of the Peace. People who were appointed to the latter positions can be seen in the *Jamaica Almanac*s and *Handbook*s. If people did not agree with the findings of the Jamaican courts they could take their cases to England to be settled. This is why certain cases have ended up in the PRO in Kew, London (see Ingram's book for sources). There are also some court cases of Jamaicans in the Scottish record office.

People in Jamaica in the eighteenth century were particularly litigious about land and property and often because of debts, which eventually had to be settled in court, did not go back home with large fortunes. The lawyers got their fees. Disputes also arose about slaves and deeds of slaves and wills involving slaves, so although it is difficult to find the relevant cases, these records should not be overlooked by those seeking African ancestors. Runaway slaves were also likely to end up as court cases if their ownership was disputed. E. Braithwaite in *The Development of the Creole Society in Jamaica, 1770-1820* (Oxford: Clarendon Press, 1971, 374 pp.) has an excellent section on the courts as well as an appendix on the Slave Laws passed in Jamaica, 1770-1820. The rights of free coloured people in court are also covered.

Court of Chancery

Court of Chancery records exist in the Jamaican Archives from about 1672 to 1879 (Ref. 1B/11). They are enrolled in about 900 volumes, of which the largest 608 are general proceedings which include bills, answers, demurrers, petitions, masters' reports and decrees, 1672-1876. There are also decrees, minute and order books, fee and file books, masters' reports, 1783-1869 (136 volumes), petitions and recognizances and indexes to some of the proceedings. There has been no inventory made of this collection but a 1938 article is believed to be reliable by Ingram: "Notes on the Record of the Supreme Court, the Chancery and Vice-Admiralty Courts of Jamaica" by Agnes M. Butterfield (*Bulletin of the Institute of Historical Research*, Vol. XVI, No. 47, November 1938, pp. 88-99). A copy is found in the RCS library. There are also typescript indexes to chancery proceedings, 1787 to May 1827, giving the names of principal parties to suits, in 30 index binders.

Supreme Court

About 800 volumes of Supreme Court records exist, from 1680 to 1894 in the Jamaican RGO (Ref. 1B/11). These include judgments, hurry books, assignment books, minute books, order books and also vendition, receipt and summons books and some letter books of the provost marshall in the 1800s, judgments of the assize courts, the circuit courts books of patents for pardons 1848-1861, general indexes, 1750-1857, 18 volumes. For a more complete description see Ingram, page 549, and the reference by Butterfield for chancery records. Middlesex County did not have an assize court; the relevant cases were tried in Spanish Town in the all-island courts.

Grand Court or Court of Error

There are twelve volumes from this court and the proceedings exist in the Jamaican RGO from 1709-1752 and 1784-1838 (Ref. 1B/11).

Court of the Ordinary

The last court is the Court of the Ordinary, which also had a small court with 19 volumes from 1760-1879, with four boxes of additional proceedings in the Jamaica RGO (Ref. 1B/11). The records include Citations 1764-1862, Proceedings 1785-1854 and Orders 1796-1878.

In addition to the courts of Hanover, St. James and St. Andrew, K. E. Ingram (*Sources of Jamaican History, 1655-1838: A Bibliographical Survey with Particular Reference to Manuscript Sources*, London: Inter Documentation Company, UK Ltd., 1976, 2 vols., 1310 pp.) also lists and describes several specific cases and opinions which exist in manuscript form in various repositories (pp. 555-567). Powers of Attorney collections are also listed (pp. 569-70).

There are no means to access the records in this section other than in Jamaica, and as far as I know they have not been microfilmed. Patricia Jackson on her site lists some laws particularly related to slavery. See her home page for more detail. http://jamaicanfamilysearch.com/

Newspapers

General Sources

Newspapers are useful to the genealogist, because they give the flavour of the times. You can read what your ancestor was reading when he or she lived. The two Jamaican papers that I have researched are *The Daily Gleaner* and *The Royal Gazette*, but there are several others. Both of these in addition to advertizing and general news also give vital records, births, deaths, marriages and obituaries. I have in fact done some extraction of the vital records from *The Daily Gleaner* from microfilms from 1865-1940; however, this is not a completed project at this time. E. Braithwaite discusses the press and lists many current newspapers in *The Development of the Creole Society in Jamaica, 1770-1820* (Oxford: Clarendon Press, 1971, 374 pp.)

The Library of Congress, Washington D.C., has many Jamaican newspapers in its library, and the Newspaper Library of the British Library at Colindale Ave, London, has Jamaican newspapers. Some of these are the originals and some are on microfilm. The largest collection, however, is in the National Library of Jamaica, encompassed in the West India Reference Library. These are the originals and are sometimes in fragile condition. Also they are dusty, dirty and cumbersome to handle. If you can obtain them on microfilm it makes them much easier to use. K. E. Ingram in his book, *Sources of Jamaican History, 1655-1838: A Bibliographical Survey with Particular Reference to Manuscript Sources* (London: Inter Documentation Company, UK Ltd., 1976, 2 vols., 1310 pp.), discusses the availability of many Jamaican newspapers (pp. 157 to 164). A good overview of Jamaican newspapers available in the NLJ is given in "Jamaican Newspapers of the 18th, Early 19th Centuries" by Rema Reckford (*Jamaica Historical Society Bulletin*, Vol. 5, Nos. 14, 15 & 16, pp. 189-191, 1972).

Microfilm

For those who are not likely to get to Washington D.C. or London, consider the possibility of obtaining newspapers on microfilm via interlibrary loan. A book which lists microform newspapers in print is available in many reference sections of libraries, e.g. *Newspapers in Microform* (Ann Arbor, MI: UMI, c.1995, LC number: Z6946.S48x). The international section lists those which are available for Jamaica. While they are not as complete as the collection in Jamaica, they are more available and easier to use if you have access to a microfilm reader.

The Collindale newspaper library (British Library) can be searched on line at http://www.bl.uk/catalogues/newspapers/. The Library of Congress http://catalog Look for the *Daily Gleaner* and De Cordova's Advertising Sheet. listing for early issues. The New York Public Library also has some microfilm of *The Daily Gleaner* from December 1899 to the present http://catnyp.nypl.org/. This is the search page for the catalog. Under title put in Gleaner or Daily Gleaner. The call number for the microfilm is: Sc Micro RS-14.loc.gov/ is more difficult to search for Jamaican Newspapers but it has a run of the Daily Gleaner #457 on Microfilm in its catalog.

On Line Archives

The Daily Gleaner is now on line as an archive. http://gleaner.newspaperarchive.com/ Although the dates begin from 1834 when the Gleaner was first printed there are very few issues until 1865 during the time of the Morant Bay Rebellion when papers were kept. This site is a pay site but it allows you to browse as well as find specific days. In 2006 it cost US$49.95 for a year. There is also a search function where you can put in your family surname and see when the family name appeared in the Gleaner. You can get a print out of the article. There are some months missing from some years, and some issues only contain 1 page. You need Adobe Reader to access this site as well as your browser.

Patricia Jackson also has excerpts from the *Daily Gleaner* and other newspapers such as the *Royal Gazette*, *The Falmouth Post*, the *Jamaica Courant*, the *Jamaica Witness* etc. Some of the pages are free to all, others are for members only. In 2006, it cost US $8.00 for a month to become a member. http://jamaicanfamilysearch.com/

Occupations

This is a section in which I have not done a lot of research at present, but those references which I have found on occupations in Jamaica are listed here. It is interesting that I have found no books so far on Lawyers/Attorneys, though the lawyers were quite plentiful in eighteenth century Jamaica. (Lists of people who read for the Bar from the Courts of Law, London, might yield some information on Jamaican law graduates.)

Printers and Printing in Jamaica

Cundall has written an article on the printers and printing press in Jamaica: "The Press and Printers of Jamaica prior to 1820" by F. Cundall (*Proceedings of American Antique Society*, Vol. 26, pp. 290-412, 1916). A copy of this is in the RCS library. Another article source is "Early Jamaican Printing" by Glory Robertson (*Jamaica Journal*, Vol. 3, No. 4, pp. 7-11, 1969). A reprint of a *Daily Gleaner* article by F. Cundall can be found in the RCS library: "A History of Printing in Jamaica from 1717 to 1834" (reprinted in the Centenary number of the *Gleaner*, September 13, 1934, 63 pp., Kingston, Jamaica).

Policemen

According to my mother, many Irishmen came to Jamaica as policemen. A reference on policemen found in the RCS library is H. T. Thomas' "The story of a West Indian Policeman or Forty-Seven years in the Jamaica Constabulary" (Kingston, Jamaica, 1927, 416 pp.). I don't know if this story is about an Irishman.

Photographers

There have been several well-known photographers in Jamaica, who are described in "History of Photography in Jamaica 1840-1910" by David Lumsden (*Jamaican Historical Society Bulletin*, Vol. 9, Nos. 12 & 13, pp. 191-198, 1988).

Surveyors

As mentioned before, the book *Jamaica Surveyed: Plantation maps and plans of the eighteenth and nineteenth centuries* by B. W. Higman (Kingston, Jamaica: Institute of Jamaica Publications Ltd., 1988, 307 pp.) has good information on surveyors and their relationships with each other as in business.

Clergymen

The life led by an Anglican and Baptist minister respectively are found in: "Memoir of George William Downer: Archdeacon of Surrey and Rector of Kingston, 1883-1912" by Lindsay P. Downer (*Jamaican Historical Society Bulletin*, Vol. 9, Nos. 10 & 11, pp. 160-175, 1987), and "Memories of my Life in Jamaica" by Inez K. Sibley (*Jamaican Historical Society Bulletin*, Vol. 9, No. 5, pp. 100-105, 1986). Inez was the daughter of a Baptist minister and granddaughter of Reverend Knibb, a famous Baptist minister. "A List of Emigrant Ministers to America, 1690-1811" by Gerald Fothergill (Heritage Books, Maryland, ISBN 0-7884-2153-0) has some Jamaican Anglican Ministers listed as well as those who went to other West Indian Islands. The materials for the list were derived from Money Books, King's Warrant Books, Treasury Papers, and Exchequer of Receipt Papers from the PRO/TNA.

Planters

Some of these are covered in the History section (e.g. Monk Lewis and Thomas Thistlewood), but an article found in the *Jamaican Historical Bulletin* is "Nathaniel Phillips and the Arts of Plantership and Sugar Manufacturing" by Clare Taylor (*Jamaica Historical Society Bulletin*, Vol. 9, Nos. 6 & 7, pp. 122-127, 1986). This concentrates on the material which illustrates how good planters ran their sugar estates.

Free Masons

A book in the SoG describes the history of the Free Masons in Jamaica. It is entitled *An Historical Account of Jamaican Freemasonry* by F. W. Seal-Coon (Kingston: Golding Printing Service, 1976).

Life Insurance

A new book, called *Time Tells our Story: The History of Jamaica Mutual Life Assurance Society, 1844-1994* by Donald Lindo (Kingston: Ian Randle Publishers, 1994, ISBN 976-8100-35-4), recalls the people and events which led to the establishment of life insurance companies in Jamaica.

Orchid and Plant Collectors

On a personal note I will also mention here the *Jamaica Journal* article which reviews my grandfather's watercolor orchid collection which was donated to the Institute of Jamaica: "An Orchid Portfolio: Water Colours" by Helen Adelaide Wood and H. Q. Levy, text by Ancile Gloudon (*Jamaica Journal*, Vol. 16, No. 2, pp. 37-40, 1983). And "Plant Collectors in Jamaica before 1900: with a biography of Sir Hans Sloane" by S. C. Sinha (*Jamaica Journal*, Vol. 6, No. 1, pp. 29-35, 1972). A list in this article gives the names and short history of many Irish, Scottish, and even a Swede, as well as English men who examined plants in Jamaica.

Physicians

I include here a biography of Dr. John Quier because he not only was a physician on a major plantation (Worthy Park), but he had several children by slaves and the author was able to do some tracing of his children. This is found in the article "Dr. John Quier, 1739-1822" by Michael Craton (*Jamaica Journal*, Vol. 8, No. 4, pp. 44-47, 1974).

Lepidopterists

There are more than 133 species and subspecies of butterflies in Jamaica, 31 of which are endemic. The most famous is the *Papilio homerus*, the biggest swallow-tail butterfly in the world. This butterfly is found at the lower elevations of the Blue Mountains, especially in St. Thomas and Portland, in the Cockpit country of Trelawny and St. Elizabeth. It was first noted in Jamaica in 1793. You can read more about *Papilio homerus* in an article by D. J. R. Walker, in *Natural History Notes of the Natural History Society of Jamaica*, Nos. 22, 23 (combined), p.164. A reference on Jamaican butterflies is Heineman B. Brown FM, "Jamaica and its Butterflies" (London: E. W. Classey Ltd., 1972, 478 pp., ISBN 0-900848-448).

Besides many English and American lepidopterists who visited Jamaica, there have been some native born lepidopterists, and two have had butterflies named for them. The first was E. Stuart Panton for whom the butterfly *Atlantea pantoni* was named. He was born in Jamaica in 1866 and lived until his death in 1962 at "Hopeton" near Mandeville. He was educated in England and raised livestock on his property. He had a wide interest in natural history and was a member of the staff of the Institute of Jamaica.

The second was Miss Lily Perkins, who discovered two butterflies new to science. Miss Perkins lived at Lumsden, St. Ann, but it was during the time her father was working in Trelawny and rented Baron Hill house near Jackson Town when she discovered *Leptotes perkinsae*, also known as Miss Perkins' Blue. This butterfly was first identified in 1931 and is partial to the flowers of the Bull Hoof (*Bauhinia divaricata*). At Lumsden she collected a new species called *Phocides lincea perkinsi*, also known as Miss Perkins' Skipper. It is found in St. James, Trelawny and St. Ann.

Animal Husbandry

I knew Dr. Lecky when I was a child because he worked with my father at Grove Place an agricultural experiment station near Mandeville. He has written an autobiography of his work in developing cattle breeds for Jamaica entitled "Cattle and I: and Autobiography" by T.P. Lecky. It contains an historical overview of cattle breeding in Jamaica starting from the earliest efforts in 1910 until the 1990's. (Kingston: Ian Randle Publishers 1995 ISBN 976-8100-69-9).

Artists

Culture and Customs of Jamaica by Martin Mordecai and Pamela Mordecai Westport, Connecticut: Greenwood Press, pp 217. ISBN 0-313-30534-X is a book that will be of interest to those who have never been to Jamaica, but heard much about the culture, art, music, etc. While it starts off with an abbreviated history from the Taino to the present day, most of the book is devoted to the 20th century and is very good on developments since independence in 1962. It traces particularly the

African influences on much of the culture, but includes other influences as well. Chapters include: religion, education, language, social customs (food and festivals), media and cinema, literature, music, performing arts and visual arts. In the visual arts section many Jamaican artists are named and their birthdates given. There are several pages of black and white photographs of architecture, sculptures and dance. An eleven page bibliography and index round out the book.

Drama

The players, playwriters and plays are covered in *The Jamaica Stage, 1655-1900: Profile of a Colonial Theatre* by Errol Hill Amherst, University of Mannachusetts Press 1992, 346 pp ISBN 0-87023-779-9   illustrations, notes, selected bibliography and index including names.. Chapters include theatres of the slave era and post-emancipation theatres, players and plays, professional actors of Jamaica, Readers, Reciters and Storytellers as well as slave performances and those after slavery. One of the illustrations is of a jonkonnu music band in 1837.

Additional References

History References

If this is to be truly a family history search, you need to know the history of the island, so as to place the family in the context of the time. The following serve as a brief introduction:

- *History of Jamaica, 2nd edition* by Clinton V. Black. Essex, England: Longman Group UK Limited, 1983, 176 pp. This history covers the period from the Taino/Arawaks to 1983. It has excellent maps, is well illustrated (in black and white) and easy to read. People rather than dates are its strength, although there is a handy list of important dates in the island's history in the frontispiece. The author was the Island Archivist and the book is sold to the tourist trade. As a quick overview it sets the stage for the beginner, refreshes the person who has forgotten what he or she learned at school in Jamaica, and initiates those who have never studied Jamaican history.

- *The Gleaner Geography and History of Jamaica: For use in Primary and Secondary Schools. 21st Edition.* Kingston, Jamaica: 1973, UniPrint Ltd., 98 pp. This book is used as a standard text in schools, so it has an emphasis on events and dates in the section on history. It has few illustrations, mostly maps, one of which is a foldout 1962 road map, also a rainfall map and a geological map in the geography section. This 1973 edition contains copies of the National Anthem, National Emblems (Flag, Coat of Arms and Motto, Flower, Tree, Bird, Fruit) and National School Prayer. Later editions exist. I also own a fourth edition when it was the *Times Geography and History of Jamaica*, published in 1944 prior to Independence. There is more narrative and less emphasis on dates but of course the edition does not cover modern events. This book is chiefly recommended for its brevity.

Historical Resources

The classical historical references are compiled in this section. It is not a comprehensive or exhaustive list.

• *The History of Jamaica: or, General survey of the ancient and modern state of that island: with reflections on its situations, settlements, inhabitants, climate, products, commerce, laws and government* by Edward Long, with a new introduction by Howard Johnson 2002 London: T. Lowndes, 1774. Reprinted, London: Frank Cass, 1970. (Cass Library of West Indian Studies, No. 12). Reprinted 2003 ISBN 3 Volume set 0-7735-2552-1McGill Queens University Press: Montreal & Kingston, London, Ithaca. Also published by Ian Randle Publishers 2002 Kingston, Jamaica. The first comprehensive historian, Edward Beeston Long (1734-1813), was a plantation owner of Lucky Valley in Clarendon. He married Mary Ballard Beckford in Jamaica, although he was born and died in England. Manuscripts in the British Library indicate that his grandson C. E. Long was preparing a revised edition before he died, but did not complete it.

• *The History, Civil and Commercial, of the British West Indies* by Bryan Edwards. London: G. & W. B. Whitaker, 1819. Reprinted, New York: AMS Press, 1966, 5th Edition, 5 vols. Bryan Edwards (1743-1800) was not only a wealthy landowner but merchant as well (of White and Edwards of London). He owned Nonsuch, Unity in St. Mary Parish and Bryan Castle and Brampton Bryan in Trelawny Parish. This is also available on microfiche in many libraries.

• *The Annals of Jamaica* by George Wilson Bridges. London: John Murray, 1827-28. Reprinted, London: Frank Cass, 1968, 2 vols. (Cass Library of West Indian Studies, No. 1). A two-volume set, this history is drawn mostly from the records of the House of Assembly. It is very dry and preachy with minimal characterization of people. Its chief interest is that its author, the Reverend Bridges, was Rector of St. Ann during the abolition of slavery. He was for the planters and rabidly anti-abolitionist, which is reflected in his writing. He played a role in the persecution of the non-conformist clergy who were trying to help the newly freed slaves.

• *A History of Jamaica from its discovery by Christopher Columbus to the year 1872: including an account of its trade and agriculture, sketches of the manners, habits and customs of all classes of its inhabitants, and a narrative of the progress of religion and education in the island* by W. J. Gardner. London: T. F. Unwin, 1909. Reprinted, London: Frank Cass, 1971, 510 pp. (Cass Library of West Indian Studies, No. 17). This edition includes a 1905 map.

• *The Civil and Natural History of Jamaica* by Patrick Browne. 1765 Reprinted, New York: Arno Press, 1972, 503 pp. This history is often overlooked because it is catalogued as a scientific source. It has a particularly interesting section of food plants and animals, customs and a flavour of everyday life. A 1756 map shows roads, and settlements are shown as tiny houses. Patrick Browne (1720?-1790) wrote with the long S — *ſ* — which makes this a little difficult to read until you get used to it.

• *Historic Jamaica* by Frank Cundall. London: West India Committee for the Institute of Jamaica, 1915. Reprinted, New York: Johnson Reprint Corporation, 1971, 424 pp. I have the old copy which I got on the antiquarian market and is a delightful mix of history, travelogue and some genealogy. It is arranged by parish. Cundall deals with the History from the Spaniards to 1915 when he visits a parish. He then tells of the places of historic interest. Often this includes the church and description of the monuments to which genealogies are added. There is liberal quotation from old documents. There are explanations of the origin of some place names. The book is illustrated in black and white with prints and sketches. It has a good index. Frank Cundall was instrumental in building up the Institute of Jamaica, so he had access to some of the really valuable references for Jamaican History prior to the beginning of the 20th century. Copies of this history are available from several places, including the SoG and the Cambridge University library. A review and update by Dr. David Buisseret may be seen in the *Jamaica Journal*, called "Historic Jamaica, Revisited" (Vol. 6, No. 1, 1972).

Some sources of particular times:

• *Jamaica under the Spaniards abstracted from the archives of Seville* by Frank Cundall, translated by Joseph L. Pietersz. Kingston: Institute of Jamaica, 1919, 115 pp. See also: under Taino/Arawaks.

•*Spanish Jamaica* by Francisco Morales Padron (translated by Patrick Bryan) Kingston: Ian Randle Publishers 2003 400pp, ISBN (US) 0-9742155-0-3 (Jamaica) 076-637-146-6

• *The English conquest of Jamaica: an account of what happened in the island of Jamaica, from May 20 of the year 1655, when the English laid siege to it, up to July 3 of the year 1656* by Captain Julian de Castilla. London: Offices of the Society, 1923, 32 pp.

• *The Buccaneers of America: a true account of the most remarkable assaults committed of late years upon the coasts of the West Indies by the Buccaneers of Jamaica and Tortuga (both English and French)* by John Esquemeling, with a new introduction by Percy G. Adams. New York: Dover Publications, 1967, 506 pp. Originally published in 1678 and a new edition republished in 1893, this is a major source on buccaneers.

• *The Buccaneers in the West Indies in the XVII Century* by C. H. Haring. Hamden, Connecticut: Archon Books, 1966, 298 pp.

• *Sir Henry Morgan: Buccaneer and Governor* by W. Adolophe Roberts. Kingston: Pioneer Press, 1952, 165 pp. This little paperback published in 1952 is probably out of print, however it might be available from libraries. It starts with the sentence, "Sir Henry Morgan rose in five years from obscurity to be lord of the buccaneers that scourged the Spanish Main". He lived in Port Royal so there is a short description of the town in the 17th century.(The wickedest city in the World) He was born of Welsh stock in the year 1635 and died aged 53 years in Jamaica. He rose to be Lt-Governor of Jamaica after he stopped bucaneering. He had no descendants but left his estate to his wife's nephew, the Byndloss family on the condition that he take the name of Morgan. The Morgan-Byndloss name only survived in Jamaica up to 1755. The book has several illustrations in black and white but no index.

• *The History of the Maroons from their origin to the establishment of their chief tribe at Sierra Leone including the expedition to Cuba for the purpose of procuring Spanish chasseurs and the state of the island of Jamaica for the last ten years with a succinct history of the island previous to that period* by R. C. Dallas. London: Longman & Rees, 1803. Reprinted, London: Frank Cass, 1968, 2 vols. (Cass Library of West Indian Studies, No. 5).

•*The Iron Thorn: The Defeat of the British by the Jamaican Maroons* by Carey Robinson Kingston: LMH Publishing, 1993 pp 273, ISBN 976-610-159-0 This account of the two Maroon wars is taken from first hand accounts and written in a very personable way. Thus you feel you know the person being described whether Maroon or British. Since these battles were the only wars fought on Jamaican soil, they are interesting. The sympathies of the writer lie with the Maroons and many aspects deal with their bravery and betrayal. The narrative also deals with the final banishment to Nova Scotia and eventually the transfer to Sierra Leone in 1800. Since there are some in the island who can claim descent from the Maroons, this is a great addition to family history. Several drawings, prints from paintings and maps in black and white illustrate this book.

See also: the Maroons.

•*The Spanish Town Papers: some sidelights on the American war of Independence* by E. Arnot Robertson. New York: The Macmillan Company 1959 illustrations of letters, no bibliography or index, 2 Appendixes, 199 pp. These papers were ships records of seized ships during the American Independence war in Kingston, Jamaica and include some letters. Not much of Jamaican's but more as a flavour of the times in the 1779-80's. This book could be republished with a good name index.

Life for blacks and whites on the plantations is covered in the following books:

• *Journal of a West-India proprietor, kept during a residence in the Island of Jamaica* by the late Matthew Gregory Lewis (also known as Monk Lewis). London: J. Murray, 1834, 408 pp. Oxford: Oxford University Press, reprint paperback 1999, pp 294   ISBN 0--19-28326-1For a first hand account of life on a plantation in 1815-8, this book is especially valuable. Monk Lewis (1775-1818) was known for the novel he authored and tried to improve the living and working conditions of the slaves on his two plantations, one in St Thomas in the East and the other in Westmoreland. He was judged a humane slave holder however he leaves out of the chronicle things which bring him less credit. This Oxford University Press edition is well documented and a map shows the location of the plantations.

• *In Miserable Slavery: Thomas Thistlewood in Jamaica, 1750-86* by Douglas Hall. London: Macmillan Publishers, 1989, 332 pp. Thomas Thistlewood's diaries have been extracted by Professor Hall, showing the lives of slaves on a small plantation in Westmoreland. Not for the faint-hearted, this is harsh realism.

• A new interpretation of Thistlewood is: *Mastery, Tyranny, & Desire: Thomas Thistlewood and His Slaves in the Anglo-Jamaican World* by Trevor Burnard. Chapel Hill & London: The University of North Carolina Press 2004, 320pp ISBN 0-8078-5525-1. This book gives insight into the way slave society altered the behaviour of whites as well as slaves.

• *A Jamaican Plantation: the history of Worthy Park 1670-1970* by Michael Craton and James Walvin. Toronto: University of Toronto Press, 1970, 344 pp. Worthy Park is a sugar plantation in St. John's district of St. Catherine. Contains genealogical information on the Price family, as well as the life of slaves and landowners continuously for 300 years.

• *Lady Nugent's Journal of her residence in Jamaica from 1801 to 1805. A new and revised edition* by Philip Wright. Kingston, Jamaica: Institute of Jamaica, 1966, 331 pp. Lady Maria Nugent was the wife of a governor of Jamaica, so was involved with the events of the Napoleonic Wars as they affected Jamaica, chiefly the changes in Haiti or St. Domingue. Her journal reveals her concern for the health of her children and husband in Jamaica and her disdain for the slothful clergymen she met in her trip around the island. She was a great name-dropper so the name index in this edition of the book is very useful to family historians. The front and back covers are maps drawn by Robertson, 1804. Some Hakewill prints of the plantations she visited on her trip are included in this edition.

• *A view of the Past and Present State of the Island of Jamaica: with remarks on the moral and physical condition of the slaves, and on the abolition of Slavery in the Colonies* by John Stewart. Edinburgh: Oliver & Boyd, 1823, 363 pp. (copy in the Washington State University Library, I do not know if it has been reprinted).

• Also *An Account of Jamaica and its Inhabitants* by A Gentleman Long resident in the West Indies [John Stewart] London: Longman,

Hurst, Rees, and Orme 1808 , Reprinted 1971, 305 pp Freeport : New York Books for Libraries Press ISBN 0-8369-8815-9

• *The Development of Creole Society in Jamaica 1770-1820* by Kamau Braithwaite. 2005, 400pp ISBN 976-637-219-5

After slavery was abolished in 1834, many traveled to Jamaica and published books on their observations. Although these personal experiences are enlightening as to general history, the authors followed the custom of the day and discussed people they met as " Mr. B..." or "an apprentice J..." which is not very helpful to the genealogist. Some examples:

• *A Twelve Month's Residence in the West Indies, during the Transition from Slavery to Apprenticeship: with incidental notices of the state of society, prospects, and natural resources of Jamaica and other Islands* by Richard Robert Madden (1798-1886). Westport, Connecticut: Negro Universities Press, 1970.

• *Jamaica, as it was, as it is, and as it may be... by a retired military officer* by Bernard Martin Sr. New York: Negro Universities Press, 1969, 312 pp.

• *A winter in the West Indies, described in familiar letters to Henry Clay of Kentucky, 2nd Edition* by Joseph John Gurney (1788-1847). New York: Negro Universities Press, 1969, 282 pp.

• *Jamaica: its past and present state* by James Mursell Phillippo (1798-1879). London: Dawsons, 1969, 488 pp.

• *Jamaica in 1850: or, The Effects of Sixteen Years of Freedom on a slave Colony* by John Bigelow (1817-1911). Westport, Connecticut: Negro Universities Press, 1970, 214 pp. Reprinted 2006

The Morant Bay Rebellion of 1865 is also covered well. (My great-grandfather William Clarke Murray was the Methodist Minister at Bath, St. Thomas, when it happened.) See also Newspapers, the *Daily Gleaner* of 1865 for eyewitness accounts.

• *'The Killing Time': The Morant Bay Rebellion in Jamaica* by Gad Heuman. Knoxville, TN: University of Tennessee Press, 1994, 199 pp., ISBN 0-87049-852-5.

• *The Tragedy of Morant Bay* by Edward B. Underhill. London: Alexander & Shepheard, 1895. Reprinted, Freeport, New York: Books For Libraries Press, 1971, 219 pp.

• *The Life of George William Gordon* by Ansell Hart. Kingston, Jamaica: Institute of Jamaica, 1971, 144 pp. (Cultural Heritage Series, Vol. 1).

•*Jamaican Blood and Victorian Conscience: The Governor Eyre Controversy* by Bernard Semmel. Boston: Houghton Mifflin Co, 1963. no illustrations Selected bibliography, index, 189pp

• *The Myth of Governor Eyre* by [Lord] Sydney Haldane Olivier (1859-1943). London: Leonard and Virginia Woolf at the Hogarth Press, 1933, 348 pp. This author also wrote about the rise of the fruit shipping companies (bananas) in the late 1800s and early twentieth century, namely:

• *Jamaica: The Blessed Island* by Lord [Sydney Haldane] Olivier. London: Faber & Faber Ltd., 1936, 466 pp. with black and white photographs.

A history which attempts to predict the twentieth century from the past is *Twentieth Century Jamaica* by H. G. DeLisser (Kingston, Jamaica: The Jamaica Times Ltd., 1913, 208 pp.), with many black and white pictures and an intriguing section of advertisements from prominent merchants in Kingston.

With three chapters covering 1865-1971 the authors try to describe the modern era in *Jamaica: A Historical Portrait* by Samuel J. Hurwitz and Edith F. Hurwitz. New York: Praeger Publishers 1971, some photograph illustrations, selected bibliography, index, 273 pp

A more detailed study of the period between the Morant Bay Rebellion and the early 20th century is *The Jamaican People, 1880-1902, Race, Class and Social Control* by Patrick Bryan. Kingston, Jamaica. The University of the West Indies Press, 2000. ISBN 976-640-094-6 Previously published 1991 London: Macmillan Caribbean.pp300. Bibliography, index

A weakness in the historical record exists from 1913 to 1938, when the rise of the trade unions, the 1938 riots and the establishment of the political parties occasioned historical treatment. The beginning and failure of the West Indies Federation are covered briefly in the modern histories (see Clinton Black). Social and economic changes since

Independence in 1962 are chronicled. Treatment is needed on how the great Wars of the 20th Century, World Wars I and II, the Great Depression and the Cold War affected events and people in Jamaica.

One contribution is: *Jamaica's Part in the Great War, 1915-1918.*by F. Cundall, (London: Institute of Jamaica, by the West India Commission, 1925) Another is: Race, War and Nationalism: A Social History of West Indians in the First World War by Glenaford Howe 2002, 304 pp Kingston: Ian Randle Publishers ISBN 976-637-063-X   A third is *Jamaican Volunteers in the First World War: Race, Masculinity and the Development of National Consciousness* by Richard Smith Manchester: Manchester University Press, 2004, 192 pp ISBN : 0719069858

The Daily Gleaner has printed columns on line of historical interest to those pursuing the lives of their forebears. They are called "Pieces of the Past" and are at: http://www.jamaica-gleaner.com/pages/history/

Many of the above sources and additional ones are listed on line at the WorldGen Web Jamaica site which I keep at Sources of Jamaican Genealogy: http://users.pullman.com/mitchelm/sources.htm

Bibliographies, References and Genealogies

When you are looking for a source of information but it is not listed in any other section of this book, this list will help determine if any information on the topic exists. I have also included here the sources of genealogies of families of Jamaica which I know are available, although these are very limited.

General

   • *Sources of Jamaican History, 1655-1838: A Bibliographical Survey with Particular Reference to Manuscript Sources* by K. E. Ingram. London: Inter Documentation Company, UK Ltd., 1976, 2 vols., 1310 pp. I have found this two-volume series to be one of the most useful sources for early genealogy; the only drawback is that it is difficult to obtain. You may however find the volumes in some libraries, especially university libraries which specialize in West Indian history. The manuscript sources include letters, accounts, plantation records, genealogy, etc., and are so carefully annotated that it is possible to order microfilm from repositories in England without actually handling the entire document set in some cases. There is certainly ample documentation so that any records researcher you employ to access the documents should not have a great deal of trouble finding what you want. The indexes form a great name index, because many letters were written to and from quite ordinary people; they did not have to be official persons, e.g. governors, chief justices, ministers, etc. While most of the records are found in Jamaica or England, Chapter IV of the first volume leads you to sources in North America, Chapter V to those in Spanish repositories and Chapter VI to those in Europe. Some documents which occur in series, e.g. deeds, continue on past 1838 but the author states that he had to stop annotating at some point, so do not expect to find sources annotated after that date. The author was the Chief Librarian for the University of the West Indies at Mona, Jamaica, as well as Librarian of the West India Reference Library of the Institute of Jamaica (NLJ), Consultant Librarian to the Latin American collection, University of Florida – Gainsville, and consultant to the University of Miami Library. Copies of this book can be found in the RCS, the British Library, the University of Florida (non-circulating) and the University of California.

• *Jamaica: World Bibliographical Series, Volume 45* by Kenneth E. Ingram. Oxford, England; Santa Barbara, Calif.: Clio Press, New Edition 1997, 369 pp. ISBN: 0585026696 By the same author as the above, this annotated bibliography treats also modern and contemporary topics. Although only about 50 pages are devoted to historical and related books, those who want to know more about the island throughout its history, from the arts, education and literature to finance and statistics can find sources listed in this bibliography. Includes index.
Electronic reproduction.Boulder, Colo.: NetLibrary, 1999. Available via the World Wide Web in multiple electronic file formats. Access may be limited to NetLibrary affiliated libraries.

•*Bibliographia Jamaicensis: A list of Jamaica Books and pamphlets, magazine articles, newspapers and Maps, most of which are in the library of the institute of Jamaica.* By Frank Cundall. Originally published 1902, reprinted 1971. New York: Lenox Hill Pub (Burt Franklin) SBN 8337-0740X pp83   Index of Names.

• *Tracing Your West Indian Ancestors* by Guy Grannum Public Record Office Readers Guide No 11. PRO, Kew, Surrey, 2nd Edition, 2002 pp 194. ISBN 1 903365 38 4

The second edition of Guy Grannum's book came out in 2002. This was before the PRO changed its name to The National Archives, Kew, so it is still called the Public Record Office Readers Guide No 11. While this book is for the whole of the West Indies, it is very helpful for the records pertaining to Jamaica which are held in the National Archives/PRO. Specifics of the call numbers for resources are on page 144-147 for Jamaica. It has been updated and expanded from the first edition so that it is particularly helpful for the beginner and explains the Slave resources and military resources very well. In addition many illustrations of the records are shown. A section is included on the Colonial Civil Servant. The bibliography leads to sources for other West Indian Islands, which were pathways to Jamaica for some people

• *Jamaican Records: A Research Manual.* Compiled and published by Stephen D. Porter England: London. 1999 ISBN 0-9536356-0-0

This handy two part guide is useful for those located in Jamaica or England. In the first part it describes the records and facilities in Jamaica and in the second part those in England. The author has given talks on Jamaican research at the SOG.

• "Materials for Family History in Jamaica" by Philip Wright. *The Genealogists' Magazine*, Vol. 15, No. 7, pp. 239-250, 1966. This article was a talk delivered to the Society of Genealogists in February 1966, and is a general discussion of people and records but does not give a detailed bibliography.

• "Jamaican Research in Britain" by Charlotte Soares. *Family Tree Magazine*, p. 35, April, 1991. This short one-page article gives some of the references available in England for research on Jamaican families.

• *The Catalogue of the West India Reference Library.* Institute of Jamaica, Kingston, West India Reference Library. Millwood, New York: Kraus International Publications, 1980, 6. vols. This catalogue gives the holdings of the manuscripts and books in the West India Collection held at the National Library of Jamaica (formerly the Institute of Jamaica). The collection was greatly increased by the work of Frank Cundall in the early part of this century. A copy of the catalogue is held in the book section of the Latin American Floor of the FHLibrary, Salt Lake City (in the FHL Catalog, look under West Indies, not Jamaica). It is not on microfilm. Part One, three volumes, is Authors and Titles; Part Two, three volumes, is Subjects. Large libraries specializing in the West Indies might have this book. A review of the "West India Reference Library of the Institute of Jamaica" by Glory Robertson is found in the *Jamaica Journal* (Vol. 6, No. 1, pp. 17-20, 1972).

• *A-Z of Jamaican Heritage* by Olive Senior. Kingston: The Gleaner Company and Heinemann Educational Books (Caribbean) Limited, 1983, 176 pp. As suggested by the title, this book is arranged in the format of a dictionary or encyclopedia with paragraphs such as Abeng, Accompong and Ackee to YS, Yassi and Zemi. Black and white pictures are included on nearly every page, which enhances the information on the heritage of Jamaicans. A subject index is included in the beginning of the book. Her renamed book is:

•*The Encyclopedia of Jamaican Heritage* by Olive Senior. Jamaica: TwinGuinep Pub Ltd, 2003, 580 pp. ISBN: 976-8007-14-1
With nearly 1000 entries and 800 photographs it enlarges on the earlier edition.

• *Jamaica Talk: Three Hundred Years of the English Language in Jamaica* by Frederic G. Cassidy. London: MacMillan & Co., 1961, 468 pp. Because the language Jamaicans speak is endowed with words and structure from all the groups which came to Jamaica, European and African, this book which at first may seem out of context, I have found to be a great adjunct to anyone studying Jamaican family history. Particularly if you get into manuscripts and letters it is useful to know how the words are and were used in Jamaica and from where they came. Some slave names, for example, were derived from the days of the week in Africa, namely:

Day	Male	Female
Monday	Cudjoe	Juba
Tuesday	Cubbenah	Beneba
Wednesday	Quaco	Cuba
Thursday	Quao	Abba
Friday	Cuffee	Pheba
Saturday	Quamin	Mimba
Sunday	Quashee	Quasheba

A companion book is:
• *Dictionary of Jamaican English* edited by F. G. Cassidy and R. B. Le Page. London: Cambridge University Press, 1967, 489 pp.

There are also some periodicals which have many articles of interest to family historians.

• *Jamaican Historical Society Bulletin*. Kingston: Jamaican Historical Society, Aug. 1952 - present (quarterly, but may be irregular).

• *Jamaica Journal: Quarterly of the Institute of Jamaica* (now the National Library of Jamaica), 1967 - present, published articles on History as well as Art, Literature, Music, Science and Education. This journal is found in the RCS Collection at Cambridge University and may also be available for photocopy interlibrary loan from libraries such as the University of Florida and the Library of Congress. The *Jamaica Journal* articles are richly illustrated with old pictures, maps and other prints which add greatly to understanding the subject. I have used extensive examples of articles from this journal throughout this book, because I have found them to be very readable and well documented on the whole.

Genealogy

• *Caribbeana: being Miscellaneous Papers relating to the History, Genealogy, Topography and Antiquities of the British West Indies* edited by Vere Langford Oliver, Member of American Antiquities Society, corresponding Member New England Historical Genealogical Society. 1909-1916, 6 vols. Because Mr. Oliver examined many sources in England and Jamaica from which he extracted information for this work, this genealogical reference is very useful. There are pedigrees and tentative pedigrees which he evolved of people from St. Kitts, Barbados, but a great deal from Jamaica, especially from 1655 to 1800. The format is similar to that of The New England Historical and Genealogical Register, with pedigrees, wills and other records intermixed in different volumes. The FHLibrary of Salt Lake City holds a copy in the book area on the Latin American Floor and this copy has been microfilmed (FHL Film # 038848) except for Volume 4 and some parts from Volume 6 which are missing (FHL Catalog: West Indies). The Society of Genealogists of London (SoG) holds a copy and has put the book on microfiche for sale, and Cambridge University Library, England, was a subscriber to the series and holds the series in the main library. Vere Oliver had a helper in this endeavour, a Mrs. Verona T. C. Smith who kept handwritten notes and extracts of the work including pedigrees. Approximately 43 volumes of these notes were turned over to the SoG. They have been microfilmed (negative film) but not indexed in a comprehensive index; each volume had a separate index. I did not have a great deal of time to examine the films, so I am not sure how much additional information is available which was unpublished in *Caribbeana* (See K. Ingram, *Sources of Jamaican History*, above, for further information on this source).

Besides *Caribbeana* I am not aware of any large collection of genealogies of Jamaican people. (Stephen Porters Manual see above has lists of families covered in Caribbeana) There could be some in the Genealogical Societies in London and Utah. Biographies of famous people do hold some genealogical data. So if you think you are related to any of the national heroes, to Sir Alexander Bustamante, or Norman Manley or former governors of the island like Sir Henry Morgan, you may want to search for biography material.

A few sources of genealogies are listed below:

• *Sketch Pedigrees of some of the early settlers in Jamaica* by Sir Noel B. Livingston. Kingston, Jamaica: Educational Supply, 1909, 139 pp. These notes and pedigrees are drawn from records of the Court of Chancery of the island, and the *Royal Gazette*, a newspaper, chiefly from 1790 to 1825. Both the book and a microfilm of the book are available from the FHLibrary (FHL Catalog: Jamaica/Genealogy). The National Library of Jamaica holds 20 volumes of scrapbook-type notes from the *Daily Gleaner*, 1897-1947, collected by the author and used for the book. A list of inhabitants in 1670 is also included (See Lists of People). Additional manuscripts in the NLJ have pedigree and genealogical notes on the Livingstons of Jamaica and the related families of Brodbelt, Harris, Carpenter and Smith (MS 59, MST 59).

• *Genealogical Collection of Charles Edward Long relating to families connected with Jamaica: including rough pedigrees, together with original letters, chiefly addressed to C. E. Long. 18th and 19th Century.* 1 vol. in folio (219 ff.), British Library, Add. MS 27968. Includes pedigrees for families of Archbould, Ballard, Beckford, Byndloss, Gregory, Lawes, Morgan, Herring and Vassall. Also letters by John Roby, a genealogist who collected monumental inscriptions. (See *Sources of Jamaican History* above, for more information.)

• *Manuscript Collections in the British Library of James Henry Lawrence, Captain 60th Regiment.* British Library, Add. MS 23608, 1 vol. (44 ff.), Add. MS 27971, 1 vol. (folio) and Add. MS 27969, 1 vol. (61 ff.), Add. MS 27975, 1 vol. (253 ff.). See *Sources of Jamaican History* (above) for more detail. The family documents collected by Lawrence include vital records, wills and deeds for the families of Archer, Blake, Edgar, Gordon, Hodges, Taafe and Lawrence. See the index of *Sources of Jamaican History* for individual families documents which may be found in manuscript sources.

• *John Vassall and His Descendants by one of Them.* [C. M. Calder.] Hertford, England: Stephen Austin & Sons, Printers, 1920, 40 pp. A genealogy of the Vassall family from 1569 to 1920 (in

England, New England [Boston] and Jamaica); includes also families of Johnson, Maxwell, Thompson, Earle, Cooke and Calder. A cousin who sent this to me said that he had deposited a copy in the FHLibrary, Salt Lake City. One of the Vassall descendants married Lord Holland, and the Holland Papers in the British Library have documents pertaining to the Vassall and Foster families. (See *Sources of Jamaican History*, above.)

•*The Life and Times of Henry Clarke of Jamaica-1828-1907* by James Walvin Frank Cass, Portland: Oregon 1994 pp 155. ISBN 0-7146-4551-6. The Rev. Henry Clarke kept diaries, 6 volumes of them, and it is from these volumes that the narrative is derived. He came out to Jamaica from England as a school teacher at Manning's Free School in Sav-la-Mar but was shortly ordained as a Anglican Minister. He lived and worked in the Western Parishes except when he became a Legislator. His wife who was also English had 11 children and his diaries are often about his family life. One of Henry's achievements was starting the Building Society in Sav-la-Mar, although he often pursued other projects consisting of various inventions. His descendents include Miss Edith Clarke, the sociologist, and the Managing Director of the Gleaner Co. This is an interesting view of a Victorian in Jamaica, in some ways a very stubborn man, but with a good heart. It would be wonderful if all our ancestors had kept diaries!

•*A Journey Through Time in Jamaica : the story of AC Campbell & his ancestors.* by Donna R. Campbell-Kenny. Markham, ON : Stewart Publishing, 2003. 316 ; ill, charts. Donna Campbell-Kenny, an expatriate Jamaican living in Australia, has spent many years researching her Jamaican family history and this book represents the fruits of that extensive research. This is not only a family history but also a history of the island and of how it shaped the people who inhabit this account. Using original records, newspaper accounts and recollections of the descendants of A. C. Campbell, Donna Campbell-Kenny has brought to life the story of the different families with which her family is connected. It is also a history of the Rapid Vulcanizing Company, a business that many expatriate Jamaicans are familiar with. The book contains numerous photographs and family charts which help to clarify the various relationships discussed. As well as being a portrait of a family in Jamaica over many years it also serves as an excellent example for any family historian who is planning to record their own family history. (Thanks to Dorothy Kew)

•*The Lindo Legacy* by Jackie Ranston. London: Toucan Books, 2000,144 pp. ISBN 1-903435-00-5.., ill., plates, (some col.), geneal. tables. The Lindo Legacy traces the fortunes of a prominent Jamaican Sephardic Jewish family, from the Spanish and Portuguese Inquisitions, through their travels from Amsterdam to London, and then to Jamaica. The book was commissioned by Blanche Lindo Blackwell and is meticulously researched. While not a definitive history of the Sephardic Jews in Jamaica, It is a fascinating study of how one Sephardic family settled there and made its fortune, first in Kingston, then in Falmouth, and eventually in Costa Rica.

•*The Last Colonials: The Story of Two European Families in Jamaica* by Peta Gay Jensen. London: The Radcliffe Press 2005, 194pp ISBN 1-84511-0331. This book is about the Stockhausen and Clerk families in Jamaica. Two pedigree charts of the families are included

• *Wonderful Adventures of Mrs Seacole in Many Lands* by Mary Seacole, introduced by William Andrews. Reprinted by Oxford University Press as part of the Schomburg Library of 19th Century Black Women Writers, 1988, 200 pp. ISBN 0-19-506672-3 This small little book is part of the collection of the Schomburg Library of ninetheenth century Black Woman Writers. Mary Jane Grant Seacole was the daughter of a Scottish army officer and a Black boarding house keeper. She married Mr Seacole but he died very shortly after they were married. She went to Panama and some of her book is devoted to this phase of her life, but most of it is of her experiences as a nurse and boarding housekeeper in the Crimea during the Crimean war. Since there are very few books written by women, Black or Creole of this time this is interesting for the light it throws on life for many of the inhabitants. However Mary Seacole was a unique woman for the amount of travelling she did, she was also very persistant and amazingly sucessful when she was in the Crimea when she became a respected maternal figure to the British soldiers far away from home.

• I include here a biography of Dr. John Quier because he not only was a physician on a major plantation, but he had several children by slaves and the author was able to do some tracing of his children. This is found in the article "Dr. John Quier, 1739-1822" by Michael Craton, *Jamaica Journal*, Vol. 8, No. 4, pp. 44-47, 1974.

•*Devon House Families* by Enid Shields is the story of George Stiebel who built Devon House in St Andrew in 1881 and of the families who lived in the House and who owned it. (Kingston, Ian Randle Publishers 1991 ISBN

976-8100-02-8)

•*Vale Royal: the House and People* by Enid Shields Kingston, Jamaica:Jamaican Historical Society. 1983 pp 74. Vale Royal is a property in St Andrew that originally belonged to Col Henry Archbould 1669 or his relative James. In 1980 it became the home of the Prime Minister, the Edward Seaga. In between it was occupied by the Colonial secretaries 1929-1959, and from 1962 the Finance Ministers. Before it was sold to the Government in 1929, the home belonged to following families: Archbould, Lascelles,Lawes,Luttrell, Mitchell, Taylor, Bayley, Aikman, Gordon, Murray, Jackson, Scotland, Nuttall, Goegahan. There is a plan of the estate in 1813 and several pictures of the interior in 1983,some occupiers and their contemporaries. Some of the early families and the later occupants are described from sources in the archives and biographies. Sources are listed. Very interesting not only for those whose ancestors lived there, but also as an illustration of what can be found in the archives of deeds of houses and wills.

A couple of more contemporary biographical dictionaries may start you off in the right direction. They are:

• *Dictionary of Caribbean Biography, 1969-70, First edition.* Ernest Kay, editor. Melrose Press Ltd., and *Jamaican Dictionary of Personalities, 1995-96* published by the *Daily Gleaner* newspaper and available on the World Wide Web at: http://www.jamaica-gleaner.com/. Purchasing information of this dictionary is also available at this site.

Two sources by Cundall found in the RCS which can lead to biographical and genealogical material are: *Catalogue of the portraits in the Jamaica History Gallery of the Institute of Jamaica* by F. Cundall. Kingston, 1914, 30 pp., 37 portraits; and Cundall's *Biographical Annals of Jamaica: a brief history of the colony arranged as a guide to the Jamaica Portrait Gallery with chronological outlines of Jamaican History.* Kingston, 1904, 56 pp., portraits.

Another source found in the SoG is by Vere Oliver; using bookplate collections he adds genealogical data to the descriptions. The book is entitled: *West Indian Bookplates, being a first list of plates relating to those Islands* by Vere Langford Oliver. London: Mitchell, Hughes & Clarke, 1914, "Jamaica", pp. 34-67.

On my website I have a collection of family histories where people have sent me the links. It is at: It includes many families among them, Silvera ,Abraham, Henriques, O'Connor, Isaac, Leon, Lyon, Samuel, Solomons, Philips, Ayton, Bromfield, Ryman, Rutty, Vidal, Hall, DeMercado, Johnson, Wedderburn, Knibb, McPhail, Byles, Heron. Some of these links are quite stable, others I have to change periodically.

Donald Lindo has compiled a CD with many Jamaican Families from information people have sent him as well as other sources.. It is available from: http://www.discoverjamaica.com/shop/genealogy.html As a member of Patricia Jackson's site one has access to many families with information on births or baptisms, deaths, marriages wills as well as the information before mentioned like Almanacs and Directories. http://jamaicanfamilysearch.com/

Useful Addresses

National Library of Jamaica (formerly Institute of Jamaica)
12 East Street,
Kingston,
Jamaica, WEST INDIES
http://www.nlj.org.jm/

Registrar General's Office
Twickenham Park
Spanish Town,
Jamaica, WEST INDIES
http://www.rgd.gov.jm/

Jamaica Archives,
Spanish Town,
Jamaica, WEST INDIES

Royal Commonwealth Society Collection,
Cambridge University Library,
West Road,
Cambridge, CB3 9DR
ENGLAND
(Reader's ticket required. Note: while the RCS Collection does not allow materials to be borrowed, they can be copied and interlibrary loan of copies of short articles can be obtained. The main library does have some Jamaican books which can be borrowed because they are not rare books or papers.)

LDS Family History Centre,
48 Gore Terrace,
Kingston, Jamaica
WEST INDIES
(876) 925-8492

National Archives, Kew
Ruskin Avenue,
Richmond, Surrey TW9 4DW
ENGLAND
(Reader's ticket required.)
http://www.nationalarchives.gov.uk/

The British Library
St Pancras
96 Euston Road
London
NW1 2DB
ENGLAND
(Reader's ticket required, serious research favoured, two passport pictures required.)
http://www.bl.uk/

The Newspaper Library,
The British Library
Colindale Ave,
London NW9 5HE
ENGLAND
See URL above

Birmingham and Midland Society for Genealogy and Heraldry,
Margaret Street,
Birmingham, B3 3BS
ENGLAND

Bristol Record Office,
'B' Bond Warehouse,
Smeaton Road,
Bristol BS1 6XN
ENGLAND

Family History Centre (LDS)
64-68 Exhibition Road
South Kensington,
London SW2
ENGLAND
Check the FHL Catalog, as well as the Book Binder which describes the holdings of films which the reading room actually holds on site for Jamaica. There is a great deal more catalogued than is found in the Book Binder for microfilm.

The Main Library of the Latter-day Saints in Salt Lake City:
Family History Department,
35 North West Temple Street,
Salt Lake City, Utah 84150
USA
http://www.familysearch.org/Eng/default.asp

University of Florida,
Gainsville, Florida, 32611-9500
USA
(The Smathers collection at the University of Florida is one of the better collections of Jamaican books in the U.S.) The catalogue is available on the internet for no charge, at http://uf.aleph.fcla.edu/F

Library of Congress,
Washington D.C. 20540
USA
The catalog can be accessed on-line at http://www.loc.gov/index.html This source does not generally circulate books, but photocopies can be obtained, and also newspapers on microfilm can be acquired under interlibrary loan.

Internet Addresses:

World GenWeb Page: Jamaica
URL is: http://www.rootsweb.com/~jamwgw/index.htm

My home page on Jamaican Genealogy:
URL is: http://users.pullman.com/mitchelm/jamaica.htm

Newsgroup: soc.genealogy.west-indies

Jamaica Mailing List: JAMAICA-L@rootsweb.com

Caribbean Mailing List: CARIBBEAN-L@rootsweb.com

Patricia Jackson's Site
http://jamaicanfamilysearch.com/

Daily Gleaner Archives on line
http://gleaner.newspaperarchive.com/DesktopDefault.aspx

London Gazette Archives
http://www.gazettes-online.co.uk/archiveSearch.asp?WebType=0

Ancestry
http://www.ancestry.com/

A success story of Paul Crooks of London who traced his family from
Jamaica
http://www.bbc.co.uk/radio4/hometruths/0215paulcrooks.shtml

Caribbean Surname List
http://www.candoo.com/surnames/index.html

Caribbean Census Links
http://www.censuslinks.com/index.php?sid=152406022&t=sub_pages&c
at=3

David Bromfield 's Link with information about Wayne Burnside who does legal research in the Jamaican Archives
http://www.bromfield.us/

British Origins
http://www.englishorigins.com/

Family Records of the UK Government-a beginners site for the UK
http://www.familyrecords.gov.uk/topics.htm

Free BDM (births,deaths and marriages) of UK
http://freebmd.rootsweb.com/

French West Indies
http://www.ghcaraibe.org/

Genealogy of UK and Ireland
http://www.genuki.org.uk/

Jamaican Jewish Genealogy maintained by David Silvera
http://www.sephardim.org/jamgen/

British Library Manuscipts Catalogue
http://molcat.bl.uk/msscat/INDEX.ASP

Methodist Archives and Research Centre, John Rylands University Library, The University of Manchester, Oxford Road, Manchester M13 9PP.
http://rylibweb.man.ac.uk/data1/dg/text/method.html

Newspaper Archives of US
http://www.newspaperarchive.com/DesktopDefault.aspx

National Union Catalog of Manuscript Collections USA
http://www.loc.gov/coll/nucmc/index.html

National Archives Kew online documents
http://www.nationalarchives.gov.uk/searchthearchives/

General Record Office UK to order BMD certificates online
http://www.gro.gov.uk/gro/content/certificate/index.asp#0

RootsWeb USA
http://www.rootsweb.com/
Federation of Family History Societies UK Family History online
http://www.familyhistoryonline.net/index/general/howto.shtml

Society of Genealogists London
http://www.sog.org.uk/
Society of Genealogists,
14 Charterhouse Buildings,
Goswell Road, London EC1M 7BA.
England

The British Library
http://www.bl.uk/

The Commonwealth Graves Commission (WWI and II Graves)
http://www.cwgc.org/

The Ships Lists. Some early ships that came to Jamaica from UK
http://www.theshipslist.com/

Scotlands Government Source
http://www.scotlandspeople.gov.uk/

Cyndi's List
http://www.cyndislist.com/

Currency Converter
http://www.xe.com/ucc/

African Caribbean Forum
http://www.afrigeneas.com/forum-carib/

Jamaican White Telephone Pages
http://www.infobel.com/teldir/result.asp?url=http://www.people-search-global.com/jamaica.htm

African Heritage Project
http://www.africanaheritage.com/

Panama Canal in 1912
http://www.rootsweb.com/~jamwgw/panama.htm

Appendix

Important Dates in the History of Jamaica

NATURAL DISASTERS AND EVENTS IN JAMAICA

Compiled 21 September 1988 by Madeleine E. Mitchell.
Amended 1 November 1996

1494 ... 3 May .... Columbus discovers Jamaica

1655 ... 10 May ..... British capture Jamaica from Spanish

1662 ... Oct .... Population 3,653 whites, 552 negroes, total 4,205

1663 ... Year .... Jews start settling in Jamaica under British

1664 ... June .... Four hundred planters come from Barbados

1664 ... July .... Sir Thomas Modyford comes with 200 planters

1670 ... Year .... There are 70 sugar works in Jamaica

1673 ... Year .... Population 7,768 whites, 9,504 negroes, total 17,272

1675 ... 1 Sep .... 1,100 Surinam settlers arrive (to St. Elizabeth)

1678 ... Year .... Jamaica, Rebellion, caused by prolongation of martial law

1684 ... Year .... Jamaica, Rebellion, first serious one

1686 ... Year .... Jamaica, Rebellion, sanguinary, at Chapelton, Clarendon

1690 ... Year .... Slave Rebellion, Chapelton, Clarendon

1691 ... Year .... Jamaica, Rebellion, many white people murdered

1692 ... 7 June .... Earthquake, destroys Port Royal

1693 ... June .... Kingston is laid out

1702 ... Year .... Jamaica, Rebellion, eastern districts

1704 ... 9 Jan .... Fire destroys Port Royal

1711 ... June .... Hurricane, Westmoreland, property destroyed

1712 ... 28 Aug ...... Hurricane, all island

1712 ... 28 Aug ...... Earthquake

1714 ... 29 Aug ...... Hurricane

1717 ... Year .... Jamaica, Rebellion, repeated attempts, causing great alarm

1722 ... 28 Aug ...... Free School founded at Walton, St. Ann

1722 ... Year .... Jamaica, Rebellion, Musquito Indians introduced to quell it

1722 ... 28 Aug ...... Hurricane, all island, and Earthquake

1726 ... 22 Oct .... Storm

1728 ... June .... Coffee introduced in Jamaica from French West Indies by Sir Nicholas Lawes at Temple Hall, St. Andrew

1729 ... Year .... Wolmer's Free School established

1734 ... Year .... Jamaica, Rebellion, the negro town Nanny taken

1738 ... 1 March .... Jamaica, Rebellion, under Cudjoe. First Maroon War

1738 ... July .... Manning's Free School started operations

1739 ... Year .... There are 429 sugar works in Jamaica

1739 ... June .... Jamaica, Rebellion, under Quaco, in Trelawny

1740 ... Year .... Jamaica, Rebellion, speedily subdued

1744 ... 20 Oct .... Earthquake and Hurricane, Sav-La-Mar destroyed, Kingston & Port Royal badly damaged

1745 ... Year .... Jamaica, conspiracy to assassinate the whites

1746 ... Year .... Slave Insurrection

1751 ... 2 Sep .... Storm

1754 ... 7 Dec .... Moravian mission founded

1755 ... Year .... Kingston becomes the capital

1758 ... Year .... Spanish Town restored as capital

1758 ... Year .... Jamaica, Rebellion in Trelawny

1760 ... Easter Mon ... Jamaica, Rebellion, under Tackey; Port Maria, 60 whites and 400 negroes killed

1764 ... Year .... Population 166,454 (146,454 slaves)

1765 ... Year .... Jamaica, Rebellion, Coromantees the insurgents

1766 ... Year .... Jamaica, Rebellion in Westmoreland

1766 ... Year .... Hurricane, western end of the island

1768 ... Year .... There are 651 sugar works in Jamaica

1768 ... Oct .... Drought, to May 1770

1769 ... Year .... Jamaica, conspiracy discovered in Kingston

1771 ... Year .... Jamaica, conspiracy; assembly of 500 surprised by the militia

1773 ... 2 Oct .... Hurricane

1775 ... Year .... Population 12,737 whites, 4,093 free coloured, 192,787 slaves, total 209,617

1777 ... Year .... Jamaica, Rebellion, followed by 30 executions

1780 ... 3 Oct .... Hurricane, Sav-La-Mar destroyed, Westmoreland devastated

1781 ... 1 Aug .... Hurricane, 120 vessels wrecked in Kingston

1782 ... Year .... Jamaica, Rebellion, St. Mary's, under Three-fingered Jack

1784 ... 10 July ...... Hurricane

1784 ... 30 July ...... Hurricane

1785 ... 27 Aug ...... Hurricane

1785 ... Year .... Population 30,000 whites, 10,000 free coloured, 250,000 slaves, total 290,000

1786 ... 20 Oct .... Drought, Hurricane, 15,000 lives lost

1789 ... 19 Jan .... Dr. Thomas Coke, Methodist missionary, arrives in Jamaica

1793 ... Year .... Second Maroon War

1794 ... Feb .... Breadfruit brought from Tahiti to Jamaica

1795 ... July .... Jamaica, Rebellion, Trelawny Maroons

1795 ... 2 Aug .... Martial Law, Montego Bay destroyed by fire

1796 ... Year .... Jamaica, Rebellion, Maroon War; 600 transported to Nova Scotia to Sierra Leone

1798 ... Year .... Jamaica, Rebellion, under Cuffee; Trelawny, great destruction of rebels

1803 ... Year .... Jamaica, conspiracy to murder the whites discovered

1804 ... Year .... Two Hurricanes

1807 ... Year .... Population 319,351

1808 ... 27 May ..... Jamaica, mutiny of black troops, 2nd WIR, Fort Augusta

1808 ... Year .... Jamaica, conspiracy of a very serious character

1809 ... March .... Jamaica, conspiracy against the whites in Kingston

1812 ... 12-14 Oct... Hurricane

1812 ... 11 Nov ...... Earthquake

1814 ... 23 Feb .... Baptist mission founded

1815 ... 13 July ...... Fire in Port Royal

1815 ... 18-19 Oct... Hurricane

1816 ... Year .... Methodist Conference started

1818 ... 20 Nov ...... Hurricane

1818 ... Oct .... Hurricane

1819 ... Year .... Methodists in the island: 6,540

1822 ... Year .... Severe Drought

1824 ... Year .... Presbyterian Church founded

1824 ... Year .... Jamaica, insurrection: Portland, St. Georges and St. Mary

1824 ... Year .... Episcopal See established

1830 ... Year .... Hurricane

1831 ... 28 Dec ...... Slave uprising in St. James, Trelawny, Hanover, Westmoreland, St. Elizabeth, Manchester

1832 ... Year .... Jamaica, Rebellion: 200 killed in the field; about 500 executed

1832 ... 7 Aug .... Hurricane

1834 ... 1 Aug .... Slavery abolished

1834 ... 13 Sep .... First issue of *The Daily Gleaner Newspaper*

1835 ... Year .... Jon Wieson Davis lays out a Race Track at Drax Hall, St. Ann

1838 ... 1 Aug .... Apprenticeship abolished

1839 ... Year .... Drought

1840 ... Year .... Drought

1841 ... Spring .... Drought

1841 ... Year .... Riot in Kingston

1844 ... Year .... Census 377,433

1844 ... 5 Oct .... Hurricane, western parishes

1845 ... 21 Nov ...... Jamaica Railway established

1850 ... June .... Asiatic Cholera epidemic, 32,000 die

1854 ... Year .... 472 Chinese come to Jamaica from Panama

1865 ... 11 Oct .... Morant Bay Rebellion

1871 ... Year .... Population 506,154

1874 ... Nov .... Hurricane

1879 ... 8 Oct .... Hurricane

1880 ... 18-19 Aug.. Hurricane, damages Kingston

1881 ... Year .... Population 580,804

1882 ... 11 Dec ...... Fire, Kingston

1887 ... Year .... Outbreak of small pox to 1888

1889 ... Year .... Population 639,491

1903 ... 11 Aug ...... Hurricane, north eastern Jamaica

1907 ... 14 Jan .... Earthquake, Destroys Kingston/Port Royal, Loss £2.0 million

1912 ... 17-18 Nov .. Hurricane, western parishes

1915 ... 12-13 Aug .. Hurricane

1915 ... 25-26 Sep .. Storm

1916 ... 15 Aug ...... Hurricane, all Jamaica

1916 ... 16 Aug ...... Hurricane, all Jamaica

1917 ... May .... Women win the right to vote

1917 ... 23 Sep .... Hurricane

1933 ... 14 Aug ...... Flood in Kingston/St. Andrew

1933 ... 15 Aug ...... Flood in Kingston/St. Andrew

1938 ... . Riots in Westmoreland, Kingston

1939 ... 1 April ...... Telephone connected in Jamaica

1944 ... 20 Aug ...... Disastrous Hurricane

1951 ... 17 Aug ...... Hurricane Charlie, Kingston/Port Royal/Morant Bay damaged

1957 ... 1 March .... Earthquake, 8 on Richter scale, epicenter at Hanover, St. James

1962 ... 6 Aug .... Independence from Britain

1963 ... 5 Oct .... Hurricane Flora

1963 ... 6 Oct .... Hurricane Flora

1963 ... 7 Oct .... Hurricane Flora

1988 ... 12 Sep .... Hurricane Gilbert, winds 120 mph, entire south coast, 80% of houses damaged or destroyed

Topic and Fullname
Index

ABOUT THE AUTHOR

The compiler was born in Brown's Town, St. Ann, Jamaica. She went to St. Hilda's in Brown's Town and St. Andrew's High School for Girls in Kingston until she left for Canada where she attended Macdonald College of McGill University, 1959-1963. She studied nutrition at Cornell University attaining a Masters in 1965 and a Ph.D. in 1968. She became a U.S. citizen in 1974. After teaching and researching in human nutrition at Washington State University, Pullman, Washington for thirty-five years, she retired to Dunnellon, Florida where she now resides. Her hobby has been genealogy for twenty-three years and besides the books she has compiled, "Jamaican Ancestry: How to Find Out More" and "Index to Early Wills of Jamaica," she maintains the World Gen Web Jamaica site at http://www.rootsweb.com/~jamwgw/index.htm

3031439

Made in the USA